THE GREAT CONTROVERSY

IN A NUTSHELL

A very brief discussion of the conflict between Christ and Satan, especially the closing events and the involvement of the people of the world

"The whole world was astonished and followed the beast."
Revelation 13:3

"There is no rest day or night for those who worship the beast and his image, or for anyone who receives the mark of his name." Revelation 14:11

"This calls for patient endurance on the part of the saints who obey God's commandments and remain faithful to Jesus." Revelation 14:12

Maurice Hoppe, Master of Arts
Bible and Systematic Theology
Seventh-day Adventist Theological Seminary

Distributed by
Revelation Ministry
P.O. Box 184
Days Creek, Oregon 97429
(541) 825-3538

Printed by

CHJ Publishing
1103 West Main
Middleton, Idaho 83644

Printed in the United States of America

INTRODUCTION

"Before the entrance of sin, Adam enjoyed open communion with his Maker; but since man separated himself from God by transgression, the human race has been cut off from this high privilege. By the plan of redemption, however, a way has been opened whereby the inhabitants of the earth may still have connection with heaven. God has communicated with men by His Spirit, and divine light has been imparted to the world by revelations to His chosen servants. 'Holy men of God spake as they were moved by the Holy Ghost.' 2 Peter 1:21."

"The Bible points to God as its author; yet it was written by human hands; and in the varied style of its different books it presents the characteristics of the several writers. The truths revealed are all 'given by inspiration of God' (2 Timothy 3:16); yet they are expressed in the words of men. The Infinite One by His Holy Spirit has shed light into the minds and hearts of His servants. He has given dreams and visions, symbols and figures; and those to whom the truth was thus revealed have themselves embodied the thought in human language.

"The Ten Commandments were spoken by God Himself, and were written by His own hand. They are of divine, and not of human composition. But the Bible, with its God-given truths expressed in the language of men, presents a union of the divine and the human. Such a union existed in the nature of Christ, who was the Son of God and the Son of man. Thus it is true of the Bible, as it was of Christ, that 'the Word was made flesh, and dwelt among us.' John 1:14."

"In His word, God has committed to men the knowledge necessary for salvation. The Holy Scriptures are to be accepted as an authoritative, infallible revelation of His will. They are the standard of character, the revealer of doctrines, and the test of experience. 'Every scripture inspired of God is also profitable for teaching, for reproof, for correction, for instruction which is in righteousness; that the man of God may be complete, furnished completely unto every good work.' 2 Timothy 3:16, 17, R.V."

"The great controversy between good and evil will increase in intensity to the very close of time. In all ages the wrath of Satan has been manifested against the church of Christ; and God has bestowed His grace and Spirit upon His people to strengthen them to stand against the power of the evil one. When the apostles of Christ were to bear His gospel to the world and to record it for all future ages, they were especially endowed with the enlightenment of the Spirit. But as the church approaches her final deliverance, Satan is to work with greater power. He comes down 'having great wrath, because he knoweth that he hath but a short time.' Revelation 12:12. He will work 'with all power and signs and lying wonders.' 2 Thessalonians 2:9. For six thousand years that mastermind that once was highest among the angels of God has been wholly bent to the work of deception and ruin. And all the depths of satanic skill and subtlety acquired, all the cruelty developed, during these struggles of the ages, will be brought to bear against God's people in the final conflict. And in this time of peril the followers of Christ are to bear to the world the warning of the Lord's second advent; and a people are to be prepared to stand before Him at His coming, 'without spot, and blameless.' 2 Peter 3:14. At this time the special endowment of divine grace and power is not less needful to the church than in apostolic days."

"In the great final conflict, Satan will employ the same policy, manifest the same spirit, and work for the same end as in all preceding ages. That which has been, will be, except that the coming struggle will be marked with a terrible intensity such as the world has never witnessed. Satan's deceptions will be more subtle, his assaults more determined. If it were possible, he would lead astray the elect. Mark 13:22, R.V."

"To unfold the scenes of the great controversy between truth and error; to reveal the wiles of Satan, and the means by which he may be successfully resisted; to present a satisfactory solution of the great problem of evil, shedding such a light upon the origin and the final disposition of sin as to make fully manifest the justice and benevolence of God in all His dealings with His creatures; and to show the holy, unchanging nature of His law, is the object of this book. That through its influence souls may be delivered from the power of darkness, and become 'partakers of the inheritance of the saints in light,' to the praise of Him who loved us, and gave Himself for us, is the earnest prayer of the writer."

The above quotations are all taken from the INTRODUCTION to *The Great Controversy Between Christ and Satan* by Ellen G. White. Pacific Press Publishing Association.

All Bible references, except those in quotations, are taken from the New International Version.

CONTENTS

1
THE HISTORICAL PROPHECIES OF DANIEL

Three prophecies of Daniel cover the great outline of history from the time he lived to the second coming of Christ. They are found in chapters 2, 7 and 8. Below is a chart comparing these chapters and their fulfillment in history.

Daniel 2	Daniel 7	Daniel 8	Text	Nation
Head of gold	Lion	————	Dan 2:38	Babylon 626 BC
Chest and arms of silver	Bear	Ram	Dan 8:20 Dan 5:30, 31	Medo-Persia 539 BC
Belly and thighs of bronze	Leopard	Goat	Dan 8:21	Greece 330 BC
Legs of iron	Terrifying and frightening beast	Another horn; Stern-faced king	History records that Rome followed Greece	Rome gradually came into power in the second and first centuries BC

A similar chart identifying the four kingdoms is presented in the *New International Version Study Bible*, p. 1311.

The Bible identifies the world powers involved:

Da 2:38	Babylon
Da 8:20; 5:30, 31; 9:1, 2	Medo-Persia
Da 8:21	Greece
History confirms the 4th power	Rome

The Bible presents all of these powers in opposition to the kingdom of heaven and the saints on earth.

2Ki 25:1-21	Babylon destroyed Jerusalem and the temple
Da 3:19-23	Babylon threw three Hebrews into the fiery furnace
Da 6:16	Medo-Persia put Daniel in the lions' den
Est 3:12, 13	Medo-Persia tried to annihilate the Jews
Inter-testa-ment period	Greece profaned the temple during the time of Antiochus Epiphanes
Mt 2:16	Herod, under Roman rule, tried to take the life of the infant Jesus
Jn 19:1-16	The Sanhedrin (the church) and Rome (the state) united to put Jesus Christ on the cross
Ac 8:1, 2	This union of church and state
Ac 16:19-24	persecuted the early Christian church (see also Acts chapters 23 to 28)
Da 2:44, 45	God of heaven destroys the nations and sets up His Kingdom
Da 7:17-27	"Little horn" power wages war against the saints until the God of heaven delivers them

Da 8:23-26   "Stern-faced king" destroys the holy
              people and causes deceipt to prosper
              until the God of heaven destroys him

The work of the fourth power and an understanding of these prophecies was not to be understood until "the time of the end." Daniel 8:17, 26; 12:1, 4, 9, 10, 13. The book of Revelation is an explanation of these prophecies, it is "The revelation of Jesus Christ, which God gave Him to show His servants what must soon take place." Revelation 1:1. See Chapter 10, "Signs of the Arrival of the 'Time of the End.'"

2
THE CHARACTERS AND PLOT
OF
REVELATION

The Bible is a record of this world and its rebellion against God and the laws of heaven. The characters involved in the war and a brief discussion of the plot are revealed in Revelation 12.

First we will identify the enemy, the leader and his supporters. This information begins in Revelation 12:7-9. We are informed that there was a war in heaven where Michael (Christ) fought against the dragon. The dragon is identified in Isaiah 14:12-15 and Ezekiel 28:12-19 as the lead angel in heaven who led a rebellion against Christ. He was hurled to this earth with the angels who rebelled with him. In Genesis 3:1-15 we are told that the serpent deceived Adam and Eve and thus sin and rebellion entered the inhabitants of the earth.

Revelation informs us that this dragon is also called a serpent, the devil or Satan, and that he leads the "whole world astray" or into rebellion against Christ.

Those on the right side of the controversy are described in Revelation 12:1-5. A woman in prophecy symbolizes a church. A pure woman represents the true church and a prostitute woman symbolizes a false church. A pure woman or church is seen here giving birth to a child. This child was Christ who was born in Bethlehem, baptized in 27 A.D., lived without sin, and died on the cross in 31 A.D. He was resurrected the third day and 40 days later He ascended to heaven.

The true followers of Jesus are symbolized by the woman who fled into the wilderness for 1260 years. See Chapter 3, "A Study of the 1260-Day Time Period."

The Bible says that the dragon sought to devour the child at birth. A description of this attempt on Jesus' life is given in Matthew 2:13-18. See Chapter 1, "The Historical Prophecies of Daniel."

3
A STUDY OF THE
1260-DAY TIME PERIOD

We first find the 1260-day time period mentioned in Daniel 7:25 where it is referred to as "a time, times and half a time." A "time" is a prophetic year of 360 days; "times" is two prophetic years or 720 days; "half a time" is 180 days. The sum of these is 1260 days. Using the "day for a year" principle (Numbers 14:34; Ezekiel 4:6) for prophecy, it equals 1260 years.

This time period is brought to light during the time of the little horn mentioned in Daniel 7:8. The little horn follows Rome, the fourth world power of Daniel's visions. Daniel 2, 7 and 8. See Chapter 1, "The Historical Prophecies of Daniel."

This time period is used a second time in Daniel 12:7 where two angels are discussing the time of the end.

This same period is also mentioned in Revelation 12:6 and in Revelation 12:14. In both verses it follows the birth and ascension of Christ to heaven, therefore it would have to be placed some time during the era of the Christian church. See Chapter 2, "The Characters and Plot of Revelation."

This 1260-day period comes to light again in Revelation 13:5 as "forty-two months." A month in prophecy is understood to have 30 days. Thirty times forty-two equals 1260 days. This is the time referred to when the beast will come up out of the sea to exercise his authority. See Chapter 15, "The Message of the Third Angel," section entitled "What is Represented By 'The Beast?'"

It is now seen that the symbols of the little horn (Daniel 7:8), the dragon pursuing the woman into the wilderness (Revelation 12:3-6), and the beast coming out of the sea (Revelation 13:1-10) all represent the same power and the same period of history. Two more references are made to this time period in Revelation 11:2, 3. The "two witnesses" are symbols of the Old and New Testaments, or the Bible. The "holy city" is a symbol of the saints who hold to the truth as it is in the Bible. We understand by these verses that the above mentioned power will take the Bible from the people and persecute the true church who hold to the truths of the Scriptures.

Historical records are very clear that the power described is the papacy, or Roman Catholic Church. It came to power in 538 A.D. following the demise of pagan Rome. This power received what appeared to be a "fatal wound" (Revelation 13:3) in 1798 A.D. when French General Berthier took the pope prisoner.

538 to 1798 A.D. spans the 1260-year time period. During this time the papacy carried on a constant war against those who claimed faith in the Bible. She also kept the Scriptures from the people. The Protestant reformation weakened its control toward the end of the period.

The Scriptures say of this event "One of the heads of the beast seemed to have had a fatal wound, but the fatal wound had been healed. The whole world was astonished and followed the beast." Revelation 13:3. The world thought at the time that this would be the demise of the papacy. But three years later a new pope was appointed and in 1929 A.D. the political state was reestablished. Since that time the Catholic Church has evolved into one of the most influential powers in the world today.

A description of this event is repeated four more times in the Bible. Revelation 13:12, 14; 17:8, 11. This is an important historical event to help make a correct identification of the beast powers of prophecy and who it is that is warring against the saints and the law of God.

We are also informed in Daniel 7:25 that this little horn power would "try to change the set times and the laws." When the apostolic church entered the period known as the dark ages, it was a seventh-day Sabbath keeping church. When it emerged as the Roman Catholic Church, it was worshipping on the first day of the week, Sunday.

Also, the apostolic church had the second commandment as part of the ten commandments, but by 1798 A.D. the second commandment was deleted and the tenth commandment was divided into two to preserve the total number of ten commandments.

A historical sketch of this time period is given in *The Great Controversy* chapters 4-16, pp. 61-298. See Chapter 4, "History of the Apostolic Church From the Apostles to 538 A.D."

4

HISTORY OF THE APOSTOLIC CHURCH FROM THE APOSTLES TO 538 A.D.

A summary of the first years of the apostolic church is given in the book of Acts in the New Testament. The history of this church in the following years is picked up in the symbols of the first four seals. Revelation 6:1-8. We notice in Revelation chapters 4 and 5 that this message comes direct from the Father in heaven through Jesus Christ, the Lamb. This is a very important warning to all Christians.

In the first seal an unidentified rider on a white horse with weapons of war is seen bent on conquest. White is a symbol of purity or truth. A horse is nearly always used in Scripture in the setting of battle.

The second seal presents an unidentified rider on a red horse and a war developed. Peace is gone and men are dying. Red is a symbol of sin. Isaiah 1:18-20. Thus sin or error is taking the place of truth. There are warnings all through the New Testament concerning false teachers and false prophets who would bring error into the apostolic Christian church. Jesus informed the disciples of this in Matthew 24:3-5, 10-13 and Mark 13:3-6, 22, 23. The apostle John speaks of this in 1 John 2:18, 19, 22-26; 4:1-3; 2 John 1:7-11. Peter calls attention to this in 2 Peter 2:1-3. Luke speaks of these false ministers as

9

savage wolves in Acts 20:29-31. Jude identifies them as godless men. Jude 4, 12, 13. Paul makes reference to the apostasy in several of his books. Galatians 1:6-9; 2 Thessalonians 2:1-4; 1 Timothy 1:3-7; 4:1, 2; 2 Timothy 3:1-5.

A black horse appears in the third seal with an unidentified rider. In Scripture light represents truth. Jesus said "I am the Light of the world." John 8:12. In this seal there is darkness; truth has been corrupted with error. Scales are a symbol of weighing character as seen in Daniel 5:22-28. Revelation 6:6 closes with the Lamb's instruction not to damage the oil and the wine. God will protect those who hold to the truth through the power of the Holy Spirit.

The fourth seal opens with a pale horse and a rider named Death and Hades follows close behind. Pale represents death, so we see here that the truth of the first seal is now dead. The ministers and leaders have no desire for truth. Notice that the horse and rider are very strong and have power over much of the earth to kill, cause famine and plague. Here is represented a strong church organization professing Christ, but without the truth as it is in Jesus.

The apostolic church assumed authority in 538 A.D. to rule and control the whole Christian church. It systematically took the Bible away from the people, persecuted those who did not come under its control, and continued the process of bringing in error and changing the law of God. The second commandment was being deleted and the seventh-day Sabbath of the fourth commandment was being replaced by Sunday worship and Easter celebrations. Compare Daniel 7:25. See Chapter 5, "The Seventh Day Sabbath."

"Death", the name of the rider, with Hades following close behind, can be identified as Satan, the dragon. In Matthew

10

16:18, Hades is understood to be all the forces of evil. In Revelation 12:7-9 we are told that the dragon, Satan, is the leader of these forces.

In summary, the first four seals are a representation of Satan, the dragon, making an attack on the apostolic church, taking charge of the organization and establishing the papacy or Roman Catholic Church in 538 A.D. See Chapter 3, "A Study of the 1260-Day Time Period." A more detailed historical review of this time period can be found in *The Great Controversy* chapters 2 and 3, pp. 39-60.

The Great Controversy chapter 4, pp. 61-78, tells of some of the "oil and wine" that remained true to God and the Bible during this war.

5
THE SEVENTH DAY SABBATH

The seventh day Sabbath was blessed and made holy by God Himself on the seventh day of Creation week. "By the seventh day God had finished the work he had been doing; so on the seventh day he rested from all his work. And God blessed the seventh day and made it holy, because on it he rested from all the work of creating he had done." Genesis 2:2, 3.

Very similar wording is used in the fourth commandment when God wrote out the ten commandments with His own finger on tables of stone at Mt. Sinai. "Remember the Sabbath day by keeping it holy. Six days you shall labor and do all your work, but the seventh day is a Sabbath to the LORD your God. On it you shall not do any work, neither you, nor your son or daughter, nor your manservant or maidservant, nor your animals, nor the alien within your gates. For in six days the LORD made the heavens and the earth, the sea, and all that is in them, but he rested on the seventh day. Therefore the LORD blessed the Sabbath day and made it holy." Exodus 20:8-11.

Notice that this commandment begins, "Remember," which indicates that they had a knowledge of the Sabbath before the law was given at Mt. Sinai. That Israel was observing the Sabbath before this is evident in the record of the falling of manna. See Exodus 16:21-30. Verse 29 says "Bear in mind that the LORD has given you the Sabbath." As noted above this occurred at the end of creation week. That this commandment was not just for the Israelites is evident by the commandment itself which says that the aliens were also to observe the seventh day Sabbath. Exodus 20:10.

"'The importance of the Sabbath as the memorial of creation is that it keeps ever present the true reason why worship is due to God'--because He is the Creator, and we are His creatures. 'The Sabbath therefore lies at the very foundation of divine worship, for it teaches this great truth in the most impressive manner, and no other institution does this. The true ground of divine worship, not of that on the seventh day merely, but of all worship, is found in the distinction between the Creator and His creatures. This great fact can never become obsolete, and must never be forgotten.'--J. N. Andrews, *History of the Sabbath*, chapter 27." *The Great Controversy*, pp. 437, 438.

"Concerning the Sabbath, the Lord says, further, that it is 'a sign, . . . that ye may know that I am the Lord your God.' Ezekiel 20:20. And the reason given is: 'For in six days the Lord made heaven and earth, and on the seventh day He rested, and was refreshed.' Exodus 31:17." *Ibid*, p. 437.

Luke says that Jesus observed the seventh day Sabbath while on earth. "He went to Nazareth, where he had been brought up, and on the Sabbath day he went into the synagogue, as was his custom." Luke 4:16.

"The claim so often put forth that Christ changed the Sabbath is disproved by His own words. In IIis Sermon on the Mount He said: 'Think not that I am come to destroy the law, or the prophets: I am not come to destroy, but to fulfil. For verily I say unto you, Till heaven and earth pass, one jot or one tittle shall in no wise pass from the law, till all be fulfilled.

13

Whosoever therefore shall break one of these least commandments, and shall teach men so, he shall be called the least in the kingdom of heaven: but whosoever shall do and teach them, the same shall be called great in the kingdom of heaven.' Matthew 5:17-19." *The Great Controversy*, p. 447.

Also, the Bible points to the seventh day, and not to the first, as the Lord's day. Said Christ: "So the Son of Man is Lord even of the Sabbath." Mark 2:28. And by the prophet Isaiah the Lord declares it to be "my holy day." Isaiah 58:13. There is no authority given in the Scriptures for the change of the Sabbath. "This is plainly stated in publications issued by the American Tract Society and the American Sunday School Union. One of these works acknowledges 'the complete silence of the New Testament so far as any explicit command for the Sabbath [Sunday, the first day of the week] or definite rules for its observance are concerned.'--George Elliott, *The Abiding Sabbath*, p. 184." *The Great Controversy*, p. 447.

"Roman Catholics acknowledge that the change of the Sabbath was made by their church, and declare that Protestants by observing the Sunday are recognizing her power. In the *Catholic Catechism of Christian Religion*, in answer to a question as to the day to be observed in obedience to the fourth commandment, this statement is made: 'During the old law, Saturday was the day sanctified; but *the church*, instructed by Jesus Christ, and directed by the Spirit of God, has substituted Sunday for Saturday; so now we sanctify the first, not the seventh day. Sunday means, and now is, the day of the Lord.'" *Ibid*, p. 447, 448.

"Romanists declare that 'the observance of Sunday by the Protestants is an homage they pay, in spite of themselves, to the authority of the [Catholic] Church.'--Mgr. Segur, *Plain Talk About the Protestantisim of Today*, page 213." *Ibid*, p. 448.

14

For a very lengthy, documented study on the Sabbath, see *History of the Sabbath and First Day of the Week* by J. N. Andrews, R & H Publishing Association.

For more information on the attempt to change the Sabbath, see Chapter 4, "History of the Apostolic Church from the Apostles to 538 A.D." and Chapter 3, "A Study of the 1260-Day Time Period."

6
UNDERSTANDING DANIEL 8:14

"He said to me, 'It will take 2,300 evenings and mornings; then the sanctuary will be reconsecrated.'" Daniel 8:14.

An understanding of the sanctuary is the key that unlocks this prophetic time period. And the reconsecration, or cleansing, of the sanctuary is the foundation upon which rests the completion of the plan of salvation.

This chapter discusses the time factors. The next three chapters contain clear, easy-to-understand Bible explanations concerning the importance of the cleansing of the sanctuary.

Daniel received this vision "in the third year of King Belshazzar's reign." (551 B.C.) Because Daniel was so appalled by this vision that he became ill, certain portions of the vision were not explained to him by the angel, Gabriel, at that time. Daniel 8:26, 27. Approximately twelve years later Gabriel gave Daniel further understanding of this vision.

The angel told Daniel that seventy weeks of this 2,300-day prophecy were especially applicable to his people--the Jews. Using a prophetic day to represent a year as in Numbers 14:34 and Ezekiel 4:6, this time period extends 490 years.

Gabriel also told Daniel that the 490 years would begin with the decree to "restore and rebuild Jerusalem." Daniel 9:25. This decree is recorded in Ezra 7:12-26 and went into effect 457 B.C. See chart with explanatory notes below.

Seventy Sevens (Weeks) Diagram
Daniel 9: 24

70 x 7 = 490 days (years)

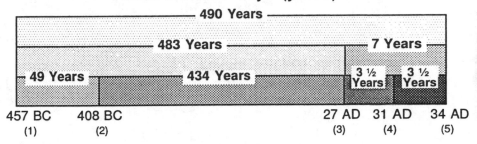

History confirms the interpretation and dates of this time prophecy. Using the day for a year principle, the 490-day prophecy, being a part of the 2,300-day prophecy of Daniel 8:14, establishes 457 B.C. as the beginning date for the 2,300-day prophecy. The ending date is then 1844 A.D.

(1) Command to restore and rebuild Jerusalem - Ezra 7:12-28
(2) City and temple rebuilt - Possible reference to
    Neh 12:27-43
(3) Baptism and anointing of Jesus - Mt 3:13-17;
    Mk 1:9-11; Lk 3:21, 22; Jn 1:29-34
(4) Jesus crucified - Mt 27:32-54; Mk 15:21-39;
    Lk 3:26-47; Jn 19:17-37
(5) Stephen stoned - Acts 7:54-60
    Gospel goes to Gentiles - Acts 8:4-40

In Daniel 9:21, 22, Gabriel completed the explanation of the vision referred to in Daniel 8:13, 14, 26, 27. The 490-year time period is therefore understood to be the first section of the 2,300 days. The dates 457 B.C., 27 A.D., 31 A.D. and 34 A.D. are firmly established in history. The 2,300-day time period, then, extends 1810 years from 34 A.D. to 1844 A.D. as shown below.

2,300 Days (Years) Diagram
Daniel 8:14

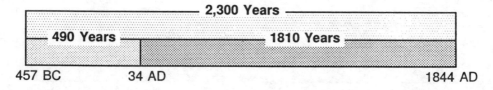

The meaning of the 2,300-day (year) time period was not given to Daniel. His book was shut up and sealed until the time of the end. Daniel 12:9.

Further explanation of Daniel 8:14 and its significance is discussed in the following chapters:

7
THE TWO SANCTUARIES

The Bible teaches that there are two sanctuaries and explains the services connected with each one. The sanctuary on earth described in the Old Testament came into being at the time God led the Israelites out of Egypt.

When the Israelite people were camped at the foot of Mt. Sinai, Moses was instructed to build a sanctuary that God might dwell among them. Exodus 25:8, 9. Instructions were also given for the size and construction of the courtyard around the sanctuary. Exodus 27:9-19.

Very detailed information is given for the construction of the tabernacle itself. The approximate size was 15' by 45'. Exodus 26:1-37. The Israelites used this tent sanctuary for their worship services from 1443 B.C. to 959 B.C., a period of about 485 years.

In 959 B.C. the services were transferred to the temple built by King Solomon. This temple was destroyed by Nebuchadnezzar, king of Babylon, in 586 B.C. Thus, Solomon's temple had a life span of 373 years.

From 586 B.C. to 520 B.C. the temple was in ruins. In 516 B.C. a new temple, built by Zerubbabel, Joshua, Haggai and Zechariah, was dedicated and services were reestablished.

This was the sanctuary that was in use during Jesus' ministry on earth. When Jesus died on the cross the veil in the temple was torn from top to bottom, thus indicating the end of the sacrificial services. Matthew 27:51; Mark 15:38; Luke 23:45.

The Jews, however, not accepting Jesus as the Lamb of God, continued sacrificing animals in the temple until it was destroyed in 70 A.D. by the Romans. There has not been a sanctuary for these services on earth since then.

In Exodus 25:8, 9 we are told that the sanctuary that God instructed Moses to build was a pattern of another sanctuary. Other verses also speak of this sanctuary and its furnishings as a pattern or copy. Exodus 25:40; 26:30; Numbers 8:4. In the New Testament Luke says the earthly sanctuary was made according to a pattern God had shown to Moses. Acts 7:44. Paul says that it was a copy of the sanctuary in heaven. Hebrews 8:5.

Daniel 8:14 said that the sanctuary would be cleansed in 2,300 days (years). We found that the 2,300 years terminated in 1844 A.D., therefore it could have no meaning for the sanctuary on earth that has not been in existence since 70 A.D. See Chapter 6, "Understanding Daniel 8:14."

In the book of Hebrews, the apostle Paul talks about the sanctuary on earth and the one in heaven. He emphasizes the ministry of Jesus as our High Priest in the heavenly sanctuary. Hebrews 8:1-6; 9:11, 12, 23-28.

Jesus ascended to heaven following His crucifixion and resurrection. Luke 24:51; Acts 1:9-11. John was shown in vision the arrival of Jesus in heaven and His appearance before the throne. In this scene John described Jesus as "a Lamb, looking as if it had been slain." Revelation 5:6. John provides the setting for this event in Revelation 4:5 when he says he saw seven lamps. These lamps were located in the holy place of the earthly sanctuary which was a pattern of the heavenly sanctuary. Thus the apostle John in Revelation calls our attention to the beginning of Jesus' ministry as our High Priest in the sanctuary in heaven.

In Revelation 1:12, 13, John again saw, in vision, Jesus walking among the seven lampstands. Revelation 8:1-5 describes another scene John saw in the holy place of the sanctuary in heaven. This time he saw the altar of incense with the smoke of the burning incense carrying the prayers of the saints to the Father in heaven.

The most holy place was presented in vision to John in Revelation 11:19 where he saw the ark of the covenant containing the ten commandments.

John describes another scene involving the sanctuary in heaven (Revelation 15:5-8) and the activity going on at the time. See also Revelation 16:1. When these verses are considered in their settings, it is noted that nearly, if not all, of the book of Revelation comes to us from the sanctuary in heaven.

Paul, in Hebrews 9:1-5 speaks of the sanctuary on earth. This sanctuary and its service was a pattern, or copy, of the sanctuary in heaven. Exodus 26:30. In Hebrews 8 and 9 Paul explains the relationship between the sanctuary on earth and the one in heaven. He also clearly states that Christ entered the sanctuary in heaven to appear in the presence of God **for us**. Hebrews 9:24. See Chapter 8, "The Work of Jesus in the Sanctuary in Heaven."

8

THE WORK OF JESUS IN THE SANCTUARY IN HEAVEN

In Chapter 7, "The Two Sanctuaries," it was clearly seen that the Scriptures present the existence of two sanctuaries, one on earth and the other in heaven. In this chapter we will learn the purpose and work of Jesus in the heavenly sanctuary.

The sanctuary on earth was an object lesson to teach us about Jesus' ministry for us in the sanctuary in heaven following His death and resurrection. To understand this, we first need to review the services of the earthly sanctuary.

"The ministration of the earthly sanctuary consisted of two divisions; the priests ministered daily in the holy place, while once a year the high priest performed a special work of atonement in the most holy, for the cleansing of the sanctuary. Day by day the repentant sinner brought his offering to the door of the tabernacle and, placing his hand upon the victim's head, confessed his sins, thus in figure transferring them from himself to the innocent sacrifice. The animal was then slain. 'Without shedding of blood,' says the apostle, there is no remission of sin. 'The life of the flesh is in the blood.' Leviticus 17:11. The broken law of God demanded the life of the transgressor. The blood, representing the forfeited life of the sinner, whose guilt the victim bore, was carried by the priest into the holy place and sprinkled before the veil, behind which was the ark containing the law that the sinner had transgressed. By this ceremony the sin was, through the blood, transferred in figure to the sanctuary." *The Great Controversy*, p. 418.

"Such was the work that went on, day by day, throughout the year. The sins of Israel were thus transferred to the sanctuary, and a special work became necessary for their removal." *Ibid*, p. 418.

"Once a year, on the great Day of Atonement, the priest entered the most holy place for the cleansing of the sanctuary. The work there performed completed the yearly round of ministration. On the Day of Atonement two kids of the goats were brought to the door of the tabernacle, and lots were cast upon them, 'one lot for the Lord, and the other lot for the scapegoat.' Leviticus 16:8. The goat upon which fell the lot for the Lord was to be slain as a sin offering for the people. And the priest was to bring his blood within the veil and sprinkle it upon the mercy seat and before the mercy seat. The blood was also to be sprinkled upon the altar of incense that was before the veil.

"'And Aaron shall lay both his hands upon the head of the live goat, and confess over him all the iniquities of the children of Israel, and all their transgressions in all their sins, putting them upon the head of the goat, and shall send him away by the hand of a fit man into the wilderness: and the goat shall bear upon him all their iniquities unto a land not inhabited.' Verses 21, 22. The scapegoat came no more into the camp of Israel, and the man who led him away was required to wash himself and his clothing with water before returning to the camp.

"The whole ceremony was designed to impress the Israelites with the holiness of God and His abhorrence of sin; and, further, to show them that they could not come in contact with sin without becoming polluted. Every man was required to afflict his soul while this work of atonement was going forward." *Ibid*, p. 419.

"Such was the service performed 'unto the example and shadow of heavenly things.' And what was done in type in the ministration of the earthly sanctuary is done in reality in the ministration of the heavenly sanctuary. After His ascension our Saviour began His work as our high priest. Says Paul: 'Christ is not entered into the holy places made with hands, which are the figures of the true; but into heaven itself, now to appear in the presence of God for us.' Hebrews 9:24.

"The ministration of the priest throughout the year in the first apartment of the sanctuary, 'within the veil' which formed the door and separated the holy place from the outer court, represents the work of ministration upon which Christ entered at His ascension. It was the work of the priest in the daily ministration to present before God the blood of the sin offering, also the incense which ascended with the prayers of Israel. So did Christ plead His blood before the Father in behalf of sinners, and present before Him also, with the precious fragrance of His own righteousness, the prayers of penitent believers. Such was the work of ministration in the first apartment of the sanctuary in heaven." *Ibid*, pp. 420, 421.

"For eighteen centuries this work of ministration continued in the first apartment of the sanctuary. The blood of Christ, pleaded in behalf of penitent believers, secured their pardon and acceptance with the Father, yet their sins still remained upon the books of record. As in the typical service there was a work of atonement at the close of the year, so before Christ's work for the redemption of men is completed there is a work of atonement for the removal of sin from the sanctuary. This is the service which began when the 2300 days ended. At that time, as foretold by Daniel the prophet, our High Priest entered the most holy, to perform the last division of His solemn work--to cleanse the sanctuary.

"As anciently the sins of the people were by faith placed upon the sin offering and through its blood transferred, in figure, to the earthly sanctuary, so in the new covenant the sins of the repentant are by faith placed upon Christ and transferred, in fact, to the heavenly sanctuary. And as the typical cleansing of the earthly was accomplished by the removal of the sins by which it had been polluted, so the actual cleansing of the heavenly is to be accomplished by the removal, or blotting out, of the sins which are there recorded. But before this can be accomplished, there must be an examination of the books of record to determine who, through repentance of sin and faith in Christ, are entitled to the benefits of His atonement. The cleansing of the sanctuary therefore involves a work of investigation--a work of judgment. This work must be performed prior to the coming of Christ to redeem His people; for when He comes, His reward is with Him to give to every man according to his works. Revelation 22:12." *Ibid*, pp. 421, 422.

"It was seen, also, that while the sin offering pointed to Christ as a sacrifice, and the high priest represented Christ as a mediator, the scapegoat typified Satan, the author of sin, upon whom the sins of the truly penitent will finally be placed. When the high priest, by virtue of the blood of the sin offering, removed the sins from the sanctuary, he placed them upon the scapegoat. When Christ, by virtue of His own blood, removes the sins of His people from the heavenly sanctuary at the close of His ministration, He will place them upon Satan, who, in the execution of the judgment, must bear the final penalty. The scapegoat was sent away into a land not inhabited, never to

25

3

come again into the congregation of Israel. So will Satan be forever banished from the presence of God and His people, and he will be blotted from existence in the final destruction of sin and sinners." *Ibid*, p. 422.

9
CHRIST - OUR CREATOR, REDEEMER, HIGH PRIEST AND KING

"'His name shall be called Immanuel, . . . God with us.' 'The light of the knowledge of the glory of God' is seen 'in the face of Jesus Christ.' From the days of eternity the Lord Jesus Christ was one with the Father; He was 'the image of God,' the image of His greatness and majesty, 'the outshining of His glory.' It was to manifest this glory that He came to our world. To this sin-darkened earth He came to reveal the light of God's love,--to be 'God with us.' Therefore it was prophesied of Him, 'His name shall be called Immanuel.'

"By coming to dwell with us, Jesus was to reveal God both to men and to angels. He was the Word of God,--God's thought made audible. In His prayer for His disciples He says, 'I have declared unto them Thy name,'--'merciful and gracious, long-suffering, and abundant in goodness and truth,'--'that the love wherewith Thou hast loved Me may be in them, and I in them.' But not alone for His earthborn children was this revelation given. Our little world is the lesson book of the universe. God's wonderful purpose of grace, the mystery of redeeming love, is the theme into which 'angels desire to look,' and it will be their study throughout endless ages. Both the redeemed and the unfallen beings will find in the cross of Christ their science and their song. It will be seen that the glory shining in the face of

27

Jesus is the glory of self-sacrificing love. In the light from Calvary it will be seen that the law of self-renouncing love is the law of life for earth and heaven; that the love which 'seeketh not her own' has its source in the heart of God; and that in the meek and lowly One is manifested the character of Him who dwelleth in the light which no man can approach unto.

"In the beginning, God was revealed in all the works of creation. It was Christ that spread the heavens, and laid the foundations of the earth. It was His hand that hung the worlds in space, and fashioned the flowers of the field. 'His strength setteth fast the mountains.' 'The sea is His, and He made it.' Ps. 65:6; 95:5. It was He that filled the earth with beauty, and the air with song. And upon all things in earth, and air, and sky, He wrote the message of the Father's love." *The Desire of Ages,* pp. 19-20.

"The plan for our redemption was not an afterthought, a plan formulated after the fall of Adam. It was a revelation of 'the mystery which hath been kept in silence through times eternal.' Rom. 16:25, R.V. It was an unfolding of the principles that from eternal ages have been the foundation of God's throne. From the beginning, God and Christ knew of the apostasy of Satan, and of the fall of man through the deceptive power of the apostate. God did not ordain that sin should exist, but He foresaw its existence, and made provision to meet the terrible emergency. So great was His love for the world, that He covenanted to give His only-begotten Son, 'that whosoever believeth in Him should not perish, but have everlasting life.' John 3:16." *Ibid,* p. 22.

"This great purpose had been shadowed forth in types and symbols. The burning bush, in which Christ appeared to Moses, revealed God. The symbol chosen for the representation of the Deity was a lowly shrub, that seemingly had no attractions.

28

This enshrined the Infinite. The all-merciful God shrouded His glory in a most humble type, that Moses could look upon it and live. So in the pillar of cloud by day and the pillar of fire by night, God communicated with Israel, revealing to men His will, and imparting to them His grace. God's glory was subdued, and His majesty veiled, that the weak vision of finite men might behold it. So Christ was to come in 'the body of our humiliation' (Phil. 3:21, R.V.), 'in the likeness of men.' In the eyes of the world He possessed no beauty that they should desire Him; yet He was the incarnate God, the light of heaven and earth. His glory was veiled, His greatness and majesty were hidden, that He might draw near to sorrowful, tempted men.

"God commanded Moses for Israel, 'Let them make Me a sanctuary; that I may dwell among them' (Ex. 25:8), and He abode in the sanctuary, in the midst of His people. Through all their weary wandering in the desert, the symbol of His presence was with them. So Christ set up His tabernacle in the midst of our human encampment. He pitched His tent by the side of the tents of men, that He might dwell among us, and make us familiar with His divine character and life. 'The Word became flesh, and tabernacled among us (and we beheld His glory, glory as of the Only Begotten from the Father), full of grace and truth.' John 1:14, R.V., margin." *Ibid,* pp. 23-24.

"By His humanity, Christ touched humanity; by His divinity, He lays hold upon the throne of God. As the Son of man, He gave us an example of obedience; as the Son of God, He gives us power to obey. It was Christ who from the bush on Mount Horeb spoke to Moses saying, 'I AM THAT I AM . . . . Thus shalt thou say unto the children of Israel, I AM hath sent me unto you.' Ex. 3:14. This was the pledge of Israel's deliverance. So when He came 'in the likeness of men,' He declared Himself the I AM. The Child of Bethlehem, the meek and lowly Saviour, is God 'manifest in the flesh.' I Tim. 3:16. And to us

He says: 'I AM the Good Shepherd.' 'I AM the living Bread.' 'I AM the Way, the Truth, and the Life.' 'All power is given unto Me in heaven and in earth.' John 10:11; 6:51; 14:6; Matt. 28:18. I AM the assurance of every promise. I AM; be not afraid. 'God with us' is the surety of our deliverance from sin, the assurance of our power to obey the law of heaven.

"In stooping to take upon Himself humanity, Christ revealed a character the opposite of the character of Satan. But He stepped still lower in the path of humiliation. 'Being found in fashion as a man, He humbled Himself, and became obedient unto death, even the death of the cross.' Phil. 2:8. As the high priest laid aside his gorgeous pontifical robes, and officiated in the white linen dress of the common priest, so Christ took the form of a servant, and offered sacrifice, Himself the priest, Himself the victim. 'He was wounded for our transgressions, He was bruised for our iniquities: the chastisement of our peace was upon Him.' Isa. 53:5." *Ibid*, pp. 24-25. See Chapter 8, "The Work of Jesus in the Sanctuary in Heaven."

"The work of Christ as man's intercessor is presented in that beautiful prophecy of Zechariah concerning Him 'whose name is the Branch.' Says the prophet: 'He shall build the temple of the Lord; and He shall bear the glory, and shall sit and rule upon His [The Father's] throne; and He shall be a priest upon His throne: and the *counsel of peace* shall be between Them both.' Zechariah 6:12, 13.

"'He shall build the temple of the Lord.' By His sacrifice and mediation Christ is both the foundation and the builder of the church of God. The apostle Paul points to Him as 'the chief Cornerstone; in whom all the building fitly framed together groweth into an holy temple in the Lord: in whom ye also,' he says, 'are builded together for an habitation of God through the Spirit.' Ephesians 2:20-22.

"'He shall bear the glory.' To Christ belongs the glory of redemption for the fallen race. Through the eternal ages, the song of the ransomed ones will be: 'Unto Him that loved us, and washed us from our sins in His own blood, . . . to Him be glory and dominion for ever and ever.' Revelation 1:5, 6.

"He 'shall sit and rule upon His throne; and He shall be a priest upon His throne.' Not now 'upon the throne of His glory;' the kingdom of glory has not yet been ushered in. Not until His work as a mediator shall be ended will God 'give unto Him the throne of His father David,' a kingdom of which 'there shall be no end.' Luke 1:32, 33. As a priest, Christ is now set down with the Father in His throne. Revelation 3:21. Upon the throne with the eternal, self-existent One is He who 'hath borne our griefs, and carried our sorrows,' who 'was in all points tempted like as we are, yet without sin,' that He might be 'able to succor them that are tempted.' 'If any man sin, we have an advocate with the Father.' Isaiah 53:4; Hebrews 4:15; 2:18; I John 2:1. His intercession is that of a pierced and broken body, of a spotless life. The wounded hands, the pierced side, the marred feet, plead for fallen man, whose redemption was purchased at such infinite cost.

"'And the counsel of peace shall be between Them both.' The love of the Father, no less than of the Son, is the fountain of salvation for the lost race. Said Jesus to His disciples before He went away: 'I say not unto you, that I will pray the Father for you: for the Father Himself loveth you.' John 16:26, 27. God was 'in Christ, reconciling the world unto Himself.' 2 Corinthians 5:19. And in the ministration in the sanctuary above, 'the counsel of peace shall be between Them both.' 'God so loved the world, that He gave His only-begotten Son, that whosoever believeth in Him should not perish, but have everlasting life.' John 3:16." *The Great Controversy*, pp. 415-417.

"It is those who by faith follow Jesus in the great work of the atonement who receive the benefits of His mediation in their behalf, while those who reject the light which brings to view this work of ministration are not benefited thereby. The Jews who rejected the light given at Christ's first advent, and refused to believe on Him as the Saviour of the world, could not receive pardon through Him. When Jesus at His ascension entered by His own blood into the heavenly sanctuary to shed upon His disciples the blessings of His mediation, the Jews were left in total darkness to continue their useless sacrifices and offerings. The ministration of types and shadows had ceased. That door by which men had formerly found access to God was no longer open. The Jews had refused to seek Him in the only way whereby He could then be found, through the ministration in the sanctuary in heaven. Therefore they found no communion with God. To them the door was shut. They had no knowledge of Christ as the true sacrifice and the only mediator before God; hence they could not receive the benefits of His mediation.

"The condition of the unbelieving Jews illustrates the condition of the careless and unbelieving among professed Christians, who are willingly ignorant of the work of our merciful High Priest. In the typical service, when the high priest entered the most holy place, all Israel were required to gather about the sanctuary and in the most solemn manner humble their souls before God, that they might receive the pardon of their sins and not be cut off from the congregation. How much more essential in this antitypical Day of Atonement that we understand the work of our High Priest and know what duties are required of us." *Ibid,* pp. 430-431. See Chapter 8, "The Work of Jesus in the Sanctuary in Heaven."

When Jesus ceases His intercession in the sanctuary above, "He lifts His hands and with a loud voice says, 'It is done;' and all

32

the angelic host lay off their crowns as He makes the solemn announcement: 'He that is unjust, let him be unjust still: and he which is filthy, let him be filthy still: and he that is righteous, let him be righteous still: and he that is holy, let him be holy still.' Revelation 22:11. Every case has been decided for life or death. Christ has made the atonement for His people and blotted out their sins. The number of His subjects is made up; 'the kingdom and dominion, and the greatness of the kingdom under the whole heaven,' is about to be given to the heirs of salvation, and Jesus is to reign as King of kings and Lord of lords." *Ibid*, pp. 613-614.

The apostle John says: "I saw heaven standing open and there before me was a white horse, whose rider is called Faithful and True. With justice he judges and makes war. His eyes are like blazing fire, and on his head are many crowns. He has a name written on him that no one knows but he himself. He is dressed in a robe dipped in blood, and his name is the Word of God. The armies of heaven were following him, riding on white horses and dressed in fine linen, white and clean. Out of his mouth comes a sharp sword with which to strike down the nations. 'He will rule them with an iron scepter.' He treads the winepress of the fury of the wrath of God Almighty. On his robe and on his thigh he has this name written: KING OF KINGS AND LORD OF LORDS." Revelation 19:11-16.

Yes, Jesus is coming again, this time as a King. When He arrives He will destroy the beast and the false prophet (Revelation 16:13; 19:20) and take the redeemed to heaven. Revelation 20:4. See Chapter 19, "The Battle of Armageddon."

After the millennium, He again returns to this earth, this time with the Holy City. Says John the Revelator: "I saw the Holy City, the new Jerusalem, coming down out of heaven from God, prepared as a bride beautifully dressed for her husband." "And he carried me away in the Spirit to a mountain great and high, and showed me the Holy City, Jerusalem, coming down out of heaven from God." Revelation 21:2, 10.

It is then in the presence of the assembled inhabitants of earth and heaven that the final coronation of the Son of God takes place. See Chapter 21, "The Controversy Ended."

Jesus, our Lord and Christ, says:

"I AM WHO I AM." Exodus 3:14
"I am the bread of life." John 6:35
"I am the light of the world." John 8:12; 9:5
"I am the gate." John 10:7, 9
"I am the good shepherd." John 10:11, 14
"I am the resurrection and the life." John 11:25
"I am the way and the truth and the life." John 14:6
"I am the true vine." John 15:1
"I AM the assurance of every promise." *The Desire of Ages*,
        p. 25
"I AM; be not afraid." *The Desire of Ages*, p. 25

Jesus Christ is our All in All! Amen.

10

SIGNS OF THE ARRIVAL OF "THE TIME OF THE END"

"At that time Michael, the great prince who protects your people, will arise. There will be a time of distress such as has not happened from the beginning of nations until then." "But you, Daniel, close up and seal the words of the scroll until the time of the end." "Go your way, Daniel, because the words are closed up and sealed until the time of the end." Daniel 12:1, 4, 9.

Daniel was informed that the greatest distress in the history of the world would occur at "the time of the end." It is important, therefore, to know when "the time of the end" is, and when it begins.

Our Father in heaven informs us very clearly in the Bible how we can know when "the time of the end" has arrived.

"I watched as he opened the sixth seal. There was a great earthquake. The sun turned black like sackcloth made of goat hair, the whole moon turned blood red, and the stars in the sky fell to earth." Revelation 6:12, 13. These same events are presented in Isaiah 13:10; Joel 2:10, 11, 30, 31; Matthew 24:29; Mark 13:24, 25 and Luke 21:25, 26. In these references we are told that these signs will come at "the time of the end" and the next event following will be the second coming of the Lord

Jesus Christ. See Chapter 1, "The Historical Prophecies of Daniel."

The question before us is "have any or all of these signs occurred yet?" Such supernatural events as these should certainly be recorded in history if they have taken place.

Checking historical records we find the following:

The great Lisbon earthquake		1755
Darkening of sun & moon turned to blood	May 19,	1780
Falling of the stars	Nov 13,	1833

For a brief historical description of these events see *The Great Controversy*, Chapter 17, pp. 304-308 and Chapter 18, pp. 333, 334. See also Chapter 3, "A Study of the 1260-Day Time Period. "

It is significant to note that the 1260-day time period terminated in 1798 A.D. which falls between the darkening of the sun in 1780 A. D. and the falling of the stars in 1833 A. D.

It is also important to observe that the 2300-day time period terminated in 1844 A. D., just 11 years after the falling of the stars. See Chapter 6, "Understanding Daniel 8:14."

11
SCRIPTURES DESCRIBING
THE SECOND COMING OF JESUS

Text	Theme
1) Job 19:25-27	Job believed he would see his Redeemer on this earth at the end of time
2) Ps 50:2-5	God comes with a devouring fire to judge His people
3) Ps 96:11-13	The Lord comes to judge the earth
4) Isa 26:19-21	The Lord is coming to save the righteous and punish sinners
5) Isa 62:11, 12	Our Savior comes with His reward
6) Isa 25:8, 9	The Lord destroys death and saves the righteous
7) Hab 3:3-15	The glory of the Lord fills the heavens when He comes
8) Isa 40:3-5	All mankind will see the glory of the Lord at His coming
9) Isa 28:5, 6	The Lord will be a glorious crown for His remnant in that day
10) Isa 35:1-10	Our God will come with vengeance for sin and salvation for the righteous
11) Isa 51:1-16	The Lord will restore the earth to be like Eden
12) Isa 62:6-12	Our God will rejoice over His people

13)	Dan 12:1-3	There will be a resurrection when the Lord comes
14)	Mal 3:5	God comes for judgment against sinners
15)	Mt 24:27, 29-34 Mk 13:24-27 Lu 21:25-27	The coming of the Son of Man will be accompanied by lightning and trumpet calls and the elect will be gathered from around the earth
16)	Jn 14:1-3 Ac 1:11	Jesus will return to earth like He ascended to heaven
17)	I Cor 15: 51-54	The trumpet will sound, the dead will be raised and the living will be given immortality when Jesus comes
18)	I Thes 4: 13-18	The Lord Himself will come down from heaven with a loud command; the dead will be raised and the living will be caught up in the clouds to meet the Lord in the air
19)	I Thes 5:1-6	When Jesus returns sinners will not be expecting Him, He will come suddenly, and the righteous will be prepared to meet Him
20)	II Thes 1: 7-10	Jesus comes in blazing fire with His angels
21)	II Thes 2:8	The Lord Jesus will destroy the "lawless one" when He comes
22)	Titus 2:13	His people prepare for the glorious appearing of their Saviour, the Lord Jesus Christ
23)	Heb 9:28	Christ, who was sacrificed, will appear the second time
24)	Jude 14, 15	The Lord comes with thousands upon thousands of angels to judge everyone
25)	Rev 1:7	Christ will come with the clouds and every eye will see Him

26)   Rev 6:14-17   There will be a great upheaval of the
                    earth when Christ comes
27)   Rev 14:14-16 The Son of Man will harvest the earth
                    when He comes
28)   Rev 19:11-21 Christ comes riding on a white horse with
                    the armies of heaven
29)   Rev 22:7,   Jesus says He is coming soon and His
        12, 20   reward is with Him

APPEARANCE OF FALSE CHRISTS

1)   Mt 24:23-25   Satan will appear as Christ before the
2)   Mk 13:21-23   second advent and will perform signs
                   and miracles to deceive, if possible, the
                   very elect
3)   II Cor 11:14 Satan himself will appear as an angel
                   of light

In order to deceive, if possible, even the very elect, Satan will
assume the description of Christ as given in Rev 1:12-16.

12

THE MESSAGE OF THE FIRST ANGEL

"Then I saw another angel flying in midair, and he had the eternal gospel to proclaim to those who live on the earth--to every nation, tribe, language and people. He said in a loud voice, 'Fear God and give him glory, because the hour of his judgment has come. Worship him who made the heavens, the earth, the sea and the springs of water.'" Revelation 14:6, 7.

The date for the judgment to begin is explained in Chapter 6, "Understanding Daniel 8:14." Other Bible texts about the investigative judgment and Christ's work in the sanctuary in heaven are given in Chapter 8, "The Work of Jesus in the Sanctuary in Heaven" and Chapter 13, "The Investigative Judgment."

The signs marking "the time of the end" are presented in Chapter 10, "Signs of the Arrival of 'The Time of the End.'"

Following is a brief historical sketch of the time and extent of the first angel's message.

Prominent men of the reformation, Waldenses, John Wycliffe, Martin Luther, Melanchthon, John Calvin, John Knox, and others spoke of their hope in the second coming of Jesus. But the preaching in earnest concerning Daniel 8:14 and Revelation 14:6, 7 did not begin until the early eighteen hundreds. In the

United States, William Miller and his associates led in the advent movement and judgment hour message in the 1830's and 1840's.

At first they thought that Jesus would come in the spring of 1844, but on closer examination of the Scriptures and the decree of Artaxerxes, they found that the correct date for the end of the 2,300-day (year) time period was October 22, 1844. See Chapter 6, "Understanding Daniel 8:14." It was understood that the message of the first angel of Revelation 14:7 announcing that "the hour of his judgment has come" was a direct fulfillment of the prophecy given in Daniel 8:14 that the sanctuary would be cleansed at the end of the 2,300 years.

During this period of the church, it was believed that the earth was the sanctuary. Therefore they taught that Jesus would come to this earth to cleanse it on October 22, 1844. The advent believers were greatly disappointed when Christ did not appear on that date.

The Adventists discovered through further study of the Bible that there is a sanctuary in heaven. They learned that the sanctuary to be cleansed was not this earth, but the sanctuary in heaven, and that Jesus began the investigative judgment there on October 22, 1844. See Chapter 7, "The Two Sanctuaries."

When William Miller and his associates first began to give the judgment hour message of Revelation 14:6, 7 and Daniel 8:14 proclaiming that Jesus would come in 1844 it was favorably received and they were invited to speak in many churches. However, for various reasons, the denominational churches soon began to reject the advent message and those who accepted and believed it.

4

As October 22, 1844 drew nearer, many of these believers were disfellowshipped from their respective churches. See Chapter 14, "The Message of the Second Angel." By the fall of 1844 there were estimated to be well over 50,000 people in the United States who professed the advent faith.

This advent message was carried to all parts of the world between 1800 and 1844. Dr. Joseph Wolff, missionary to the world, traveled extensively proclaiming the second coming of Christ. He went to Africa, Asia, the middle east, and India. In the United Sates, the House granted him the use of Congress Hall and all of the members of Congress attended his lecture concerning the second coming of Christ.

About 700 ministers in England proclaimed the soon coming of Jesus during this time. The message was given by Lacunza, a Spaniard and a Jesuit, in South America. Bengel, a Lutheran minister, gave the message in Germany. It was also preached in France and Switzerland by Gaussen.

In the Scandinavian countries the state church opposed the advent message so much that preachers were put in prison for speaking about it. God then moved upon the children, who did not come under the law, to present the messages in those countries.

This first angel says "Fear God and give him glory" and admonishes us to worship Him as our Creator and the Creator of the earth. In order for people to do this, they must obey His law. Solomon says "Fear God and keep his commandments, for this is the whole duty of man." Ecclesiastes 12:13. Without obedience to His commandments no worship can be pleasing to God. "This is love for God: to obey his commands." "If anyone turns a deaf ear to the law, even his prayers are detestable." I Jn 5:3; Prov 28:9.

History reveals a widespread proclamation of the second advent of our Lord as noted above. But at the same time unfaithful watchmen, like the Pharisees in Christ's day, tried to hinder the work. See Chapter 14, "The Message of the Second Angel."

13
THE INVESTIGATIVE JUDGMENT

The Bible clearly explains that the "hour of his judgment" began in 1844. That the judgment would begin in the fall of that year (at the end of the 2,300 years) was learned from the decree of Artaxerxes which went into effect in the fall of 457 B.C. See Chapter 6, "Understanding Daniel 8:14." Also, it was seen in the typical service of the Old Testament sanctuary that the Day of Atonement fell on the 10th day of the 7th month which in the year 1844 fell on October 22.

Several texts of Scripture tell of this judgment time. In Daniel 7:9, 10, we are given a view of the Ancient of Days seating the court and opening the books. Verse 13 says that Christ appears before the Ancient of Days. Christ is our Mediator before the Father. Hebrews 9:24.

We are given another view of this judgment scene in Malachi 3:1-4. "Who can endure? Who can stand?" during this time of investigation?

The coming of the bridegroom to the marriage, described by Christ in the parable of the ten virgins of Matthew 25:1-13 also represents this judgment scene. The parable of Matthew 22:1-14 introduces the same figure of the marriage and clearly shows it to be an investigative judgment. In both of these parables the coming of the bridegroom and the investigation occurs before the wedding.

This work of examination of character, of determining who are prepared for the Kingdom of God is that of the investigative judgment, the closing work of the sanctuary above. The investigative judgment is completed before Jesus returns to this earth the second time. Jesus says in Revelation 22:12: "'Behold, I am coming soon! My reward is with me, and I will give to everyone according to what he has done.'"

14
THE MESSAGE OF THE SECOND ANGEL

"A second angel followed and said, 'Fallen! Fallen is Babylon the Great, which made all the nations drink the maddening wine of her adulteries." Revelation 14:8.

The term "Babylon" is derived from "Babel" and signifies confusion. Genesis 11:9. The Scriptures apply this term to the various forms of false or apostate religion.

In Revelation 17 Babylon is represented as a prostitute woman. In the Bible a woman is used to represent the church--a pure woman represents the true church; a corrupt or prostitute woman depicts a false or apostate church. An application of this principle can be seen in Ezekiel 23 when the two Israelite kingdoms were represented as adulterous sisters because of their departure from God.

The relationship between Christ and His church is represented by the union of marriage in the Bible. When a church professes to be Christian and live by the Bible, but turns from truth and accepts error in its place, or mixes truth and error, it is likened to the violation of the marriage vow as in Revelation 17.

When the churches and professed Christians as a whole rejected the warning of the first angel (Revelation 14:6, 7) and put worldly interests in its place, they were seen to be fulfilling the message of the second angel. "At a meeting of the presbytery of Philadelphia, Mr. Barnes, author of a commentary widely used and pastor of one of the leading churches in that city, 'stated that he had been in the ministry for twenty years, and never, till the last communion, had he administered the ordinance without receiving more or less into the church. But now there are *no awakenings, no conversions,* not much apparent growth in grace in professors, and none come to his study to converse about the salvation of their souls. With the increase of business, and the brightening prospects of commerce and manufacture, there is an increase of worldly-mindedness. *Thus it is with all the denominations.'--Congregational Journal,* May 23, 1844." *The Great Controversy,* pp. 376, 377.

This condition of the churches was commented upon by other speakers and writers during this time.

The second angel's message was first preached in the summer of 1844 and applied to the churches who refused to receive the light of the advent message. They experienced a moral fall at that time but that fall was not complete. The work of apostasy had not yet reached its culmination. Revelation 18 points to the time when the warning of the second angel will be repeated with greater emphasis.

Says the apostle John: "After this I saw another angel coming down from heaven. He had great authority, and the earth was illuminated by his splendor. With a mighty voice he shouted: 'Fallen! Fallen is Babylon the Great! She has become a home for demons and a haunt for every evil spirit, a haunt for every unclean and detestable bird.' . . . Then I heard another voice from heaven say: 'Come out of her, my people, so that you will not share in her sins, so that you will not receive any of her plagues.'" Revelation 18:1, 2, 4.

"A terrible condition of the religious world is here described. With every rejection of truth the minds of the people will become darker, their hearts more stubborn, until they are entrenched in an infidel hardihood. In defiance of the warnings which God has given, they will continue to trample upon one of the precepts of the Decalogue, until they are led to persecute those who hold it sacred. Christ is set at nought in the contempt placed upon His word and His people. As the teachings of spiritualism are accepted by the churches, the restraint imposed upon the carnal heart is removed, and the profession of religion will become a cloak to conceal the basest iniquity. A belief in spiritual manifestations opens the door to seducing spirits and doctrines of devils, and thus the influence of evil angels will be felt in the churches.

"Of Babylon, at the time brought to view in this prophecy, it is declared: 'Her sins have reached unto heaven, and God hath remembered her iniquities.' Revelation 18:5. She has filled up the measure of her guilt, and destruction is about to fall upon her. But God still has a people in Babylon; and before the visitation of His judgments these faithful ones must be called out, that they partake not of her sins and 'receive not of her plagues.' Hence the movement symbolized by the angel coming down from heaven, lightening the earth with his glory and crying mightily with a strong voice, announcing the sins of Babylon. In connection with his message the call is heard: 'Come out of her, My people.' These announcements, uniting with the third angel's message, constitute the final warning to be given to the inhabitants of the earth." *The Great Controversy,* pp. 603, 604.

See Chapter 17, "The Final Warning," Chapter 12, "The Message of the First Angel" and Chapter 15, "The Message of the Third Angel."

15

THE MESSAGE OF THE THIRD ANGEL

"A third angel followed them and said in a loud voice: 'If anyone worships the beast and his image and receives his mark on the forehead or on the hand, he, too, will drink of the wine of God's fury, which has been poured full strength into the cup of His wrath. He will be tormented with burning sulfur in the presence of the holy angels and of the Lamb. And the smoke of their torment rises for ever and ever. There is no rest day or night for those who worship the beast and his image, or for anyone who receives the mark of his name.' This calls for patient endurance on the part of the saints who obey God's commandments and remain faithful to Jesus." Revelation 14:9-12.

Prior to studying the message of this third angel, we need to review the messages of the first two angels.

The first angel gives a clarion call to "Fear God and give him glory" and announces that "the hour of his judgment has come." As we learned in Chapter 12, "The Message of the First Angel," this announcement was proclaimed to the world in the early part of the nineteenth century.

The second angel revealed that the people in general did not accept the truths presented. He therefore described them as "fallen." This message was applied in the summer and fall of 1844 to the churches that did not accept the message of the first angel. See Chapter 14, "The Message of the Second Angel."

These two messages lay the foundation for the most fearful warning God, in love and mercy, has ever presented to mankind. This message is not a criticism of any organization, church, or group of people, but a solemn warning to flee from a fatal deception coming upon this world. God has given us these messages to guide us so that we may have eternal life in Christ Jesus.

Now let us consider the third angel's message. John, in Revelation 14:12, speaks of "the saints who obey God's commandments." Daniel, who lays the foundation for the prophecies of Revelation, also speaks of the saints. Concerning this group of people, he says: "But the saints of the Most High will receive the kingdom and will possess it forever." "The Ancient of Days came and pronounced judgment in favor of the saints of the Most High, and the time came when they possessed the kingdom." "Then the sovereignty, power and greatness of the kingdoms under the whole heaven will be handed over to the saints, the people of the Most High." Daniel 7:18, 22, 27.

John says the saints obey the commandments of God. "In order to be prepared for the judgment, it is necessary that men should keep the law of God. That law will be the standard of character in the judgment. The apostle Paul declares: 'As many as have sinned in the law shall be judged by the law, . . . in the day when God shall judge the secrets of men by Jesus Christ.' And he says that 'the doers of the law shall be justified.' Romans 2:12-16. Faith is essential in order to the keeping of the law of God; for 'without faith it is impossible to please Him.' And 'whatsoever is not of faith is sin.' Hebrews 11:6; Romans 14:23." *The Great Controversy,* p. 436.

Here is brought to view a class that, as a result of the three angels messages, are keeping the commandments of God. The fourth commandment points directly to God as the Creator. It declares "the seventh day is a Sabbath to the LORD your God. . . . For in six days the LORD made the heavens and the earth, . . . but He rested on the seventh day. Therefore the LORD blessed the Sabbath day and made it holy." Exodus 20:10, 11. The Lord says, further, to "Keep my Sabbaths holy, that they may be a sign between us. Then you will know that I am the LORD your God." Ezekiel 20:20. And the reason given is: "for in six days the LORD made the heavens and the earth, and on the seventh day He abstained from work and rested." Exodus 31:17.

The first angel instructs us to "Worship him who made the heavens, the earth." Revelation 14:7. See Chapter 5, "The Seventh Day Sabbath." Concerning this group, John says: "And I saw what looked like a sea of glass mixed with fire and, standing beside the sea, those who had been victorious over the beast and his image and over the number of his name." Revelation 15:2.

In contrast to those "who obey God's commandments and remain faithful to Jesus," the third angel points to another class, against whose errors a solemn and fearful warning is spoken. "If anyone worships the beast and his image and receives his mark on the forehead or on the hand, he, too, will drink of the wine of God's fury, which has been poured full strength into the cup of his wrath." Revelation 14:9, 10.

To understand this message, it is necessary to have a correct understanding of the symbols employed. What is represented by the beast, the image, the mark?

51

What Is Represented By "The Beast?"

"The line of prophecy in which these symbols are found begins with Revelation 12, with the dragon that sought to destroy Christ at His birth. The dragon is said to be Satan (Revelation 12:9); he it was that moved upon Herod to put the Saviour to death. But the chief agent of Satan in making war upon Christ and His people during the first centuries of the Christian Era was the Roman Empire, in which paganism was the prevailing religion. Thus while the dragon, primarily, represents Satan, it is, in a secondary sense, a symbol of pagan Rome." *The Great Controversy,* p. 438. For more information on Satan, see Chapter 2, "The Characters and Plot of Revelation."

"In chapter 13 (verses 1-10) is described another beast, 'like unto a leopard,' to which the dragon gave 'his power, and his seat, and great authority.' This symbol, as most Protestants have believed, represents the papacy, which succeeded to the power and seat and authority once held by the ancient Roman empire. Of the leopardlike beast it is declared: 'There was given unto him a mouth speaking great things and blasphemies. . . . And he opened his mouth in blasphemy against God, to blaspheme His name, and His tabernacle, and them that dwell in heaven. And it was given unto him to make war with the saints, and to overcome them: and power was given him over all kindreds, and tongues, and nations.' This prophecy, which is nearly identical with the description of the little horn of Daniel 7, unquestionably points to the papacy." *Ibid*, p. 439.

In Chapter 1, "The Historical Prophecies of Daniel," it was seen that the visions of Daniel 8 present the same powers and period of history as Daniel 7. Therefore the leopardlike beast described in Revelation 13:1-10, the little horn of Daniel 7:8, 20-25, and the stern-faced king in Daniel 8:23-25 all represent the same power, the papacy.

Notice also that the identical time period is presented in both Daniel and Revelation. "'Power was given unto him to continue forty and two months.' And, says the prophet, 'I saw one of his heads as it were wounded to death.' And again: 'He that leadeth into captivity shall go into captivity: he that killeth with the sword must be killed with the sword.' The forty and two months are the same as the 'time and times and the dividing of time,' three years and a half, or 1260 days, of Daniel 7--the time during which the papal power was to oppress God's people. This period, as stated in preceding chapters, began with the supremacy of the papacy, A.D. 538, and terminated in 1798. At that time the pope was made captive by the French army, the papal power received its deadly wound, and the prediction was fulfilled, 'He that leadeth into captivity shall go into captivity.'" *Ibid*, p. 439. For more information on the papacy, see Chapter 4, "History of the Apostolic Church from the Apostles to 538 A.D." and Chapter 3, "A Study of the 1260-Day Time Period."

That all of these representations refer to the same power cannot be controverted.

What Is Represented By "The Image to the Beast?"

"He ordered them to set up an image in honor of the beast who was wounded by the sword and yet lived." Revelation 13:14. The pronoun "he" is the beast with "two horns like a lamb." See Chapter 16, "The United States in Prophecy." "The image is made by the two-horned beast, and is an image *to* the beast. It is also called an image *of* the beast. Then to learn what the image is like and how it is to be formed we must study the characteristics of the beast itself--the papacy.

"When the early church became corrupted by departing from the simplicity of the gospel and accepting heathen rites and customs, she lost the Spirit and power of God; and in order to control the consciences of the people, she sought the support of the secular power. The result was the papacy, a church that controlled the power of the state and employed it to further her own ends, especially for the punishment of 'heresy.' In order for the United States to form an image of the beast, the religious power must so control the civil government that the authority of the state will also be employed by the church to accomplish her own ends." *Ibid*, p. 443.

"It was apostasy that led the early church to seek the aid of the civil government, and this prepared the way for the development of the papacy--the beast. Said Paul: 'There' shall 'come a falling away, . . . and that man of sin be revealed.' 2 Thessalonians 2:3. So apostasy in the church will prepare the way for the image to the beast.

"The Bible declares that before the coming of the Lord there will exist a state of religious declension similar to that in the first centuries. 'In the last days perilous times shall come. For men shall be *lovers of their own selves,* covetous, boasters, proud, blasphemers, disobedient to parents, unthankful, unholy, without natural affection, trucebreakers, false accusers, incontinent, fierce, *despisers of those that are good,* traitors, heady, high-minded, *lovers of pleasures more than lovers of God; having a form of godliness,* but denying the power thereof.' 2 Timothy 3:1-5. 'Now the Spirit speaketh expressly, that in the latter times some shall depart from the faith, giving heed to seducing spirits, and doctrines of devils.' 1 Timothy 4:1. Satan will work 'with all power and signs and lying wonders, and with all deceivableness of unrighteousness.' And all that 'received not the love of the truth, that they might be saved,' will be left to accept 'strong delusion, that they should believe a lie.' 2 Thessalonians 2:9-11. When this state of ungodliness shall be reached, the same results will follow as in the first centuries." *Ibid,* pp. 443, 444.

54

"Charles Beecher, in a sermon in the year 1846, declared that the ministry of 'the evangelical Protestant denominations' is 'not only formed all the way up under a tremendous pressure of merely human fear, but they live, and move, and breathe in a state of things radically corrupt, and appealing every hour to every baser element of their nature to hush up the truth, and bow the knee to the power of apostasy. Was not this the way things went with Rome? Are we not living her life over again? And what do we see just ahead? Another general council! A world's convention! Evangelical alliance, and universal creed!' --Sermon on 'The Bible a Sufficient Creed,' delivered at Fort Wayne, Indiana, Feb. 22, 1846. When this shall be gained, then, in the effort to secure complete uniformity, it will be only a step to the resort to force.

"When the leading churches of the United States, uniting upon such points of doctrine as are held by them in common, shall influence the state to enforce their decrees and to sustain their institutions, then Protestant America will have formed an image of the Roman hierarchy, and the infliction of civil penalties upon dissenters will inevitably result.

"The beast with two horns 'causeth [commands] all, both small and great, rich and poor, free and bond, to receive a mark in their right hand, or in their foreheads: and that no man might buy or sell, save he that had the mark, or the name of the beast, or the number of his name.' Revelation 13:16, 17. The third angel's warning is: 'If any man worship the beast and his image, and receive his mark in his forehead, or in his hand, the same shall drink of the wine of the wrath of God.' 'The beast' mentioned in this message, whose worship is enforced by the two-horned beast, is the first, or leopardlike beast of Revelation 13--the papacy. The 'image to the beast' represents that form of apostate Protestantism which will be developed when the Protestant churches shall seek the aid of the civil power for the enforcement of their dogmas. The 'mark of the beast' still remains to be defined." *Ibid,* pp. 444, 445.

What Is Represented By "The Mark of the Beast?"

"After the warning against worship of the beast and his image the prophecy declares: 'Here are they that keep the commandments of God, and the faith of Jesus.' Since those who keep God's commandments are thus placed in contrast with those that worship the beast and his image and receive his mark, it follows that the keeping of God's law, on the one hand, and its violation, on the other, will make the distinction between the worshipers of God and the worshipers of the beast.

"The special characteristic of the beast, and therefore of his image, is the breaking of God's commandments. Says Daniel, of the little horn, the papacy: 'He shall think to change times and the law.' Daniel 7:25, R.V. And Paul styled the same power the 'man of sin,' who was to exalt himself above God. One prophecy is a complement of the other. Only by changing God's law could the papacy exalt itself above God; whoever should understandingly keep the law as thus changed would be giving supreme honor to that power by which the change was made. Such an act of obedience to papal laws would be a mark of allegiance to the pope in the place of God." *Ibid,* pp. 445, 446. See Chapter 4, "History of the Apostolic Church from the Apostles to 538 A.D." and Chapter 3, "A Study of the 1260-Day Time Period."

In his vision of the "little horn" power, Daniel said, "He shall *think* to change the times and the law." Daniel 7:25. The change in the fourth commandment exactly fulfills this prophecy. For this the only authority claimed is that of the church. Here the papal power openly sets itself above God.

56

While the saints will be especially distinguished by their regard for the fourth commandment--since this is the sign of His creative power and the witness to His claim upon man's reverence and homage--the worshipers of the beast will be distinguished by their efforts to tear down the Creator's memorial and to exalt the institution of Rome. See Chapter 5 "The Seventh Day Sabbath" for information on the Biblical history of the Sabbath and the introduction of Sunday worship.

"As a sign of the authority of the Catholic Church, papist writers cite 'the very act of changing the Sabbath into Sunday, which Protestants allow of; . . . because by keeping Sunday, they acknowledge the church's power to ordain feasts, and to command them under sin.'--Henry Tuberville, *An Abridgement of the Christian Doctrine*, page 58. What then is the change of the Sabbath, but the sign, or mark, of the authority of the Roman Church--'the mark of the beast'?

"The Roman Church has not relinquished her claim to supremacy; and when the world and the Protestant churches accept a sabbath of her creating, while they reject the Bible Sabbath, they virtually admit this assumption." *Ibid*, p. 448.

"Romanists declare that 'the observance of Sunday by the Protestants is an homage they pay, in spite of themselves, to the authority of the [Catholic] Church.'--Mgr. Segur, *Plain Talk About the Protestantism of Today*, page 213. The enforcement of Sundaykeeping on the part of Protestant churches is an enforcement of the worship of the papacy--of the beast. Those who, understanding the claims of the fourth commandment, choose to observe the false instead of the true Sabbath are thereby paying homage to that power by which alone it is commanded. But in the very act of enforcing a religious duty by secular power, the churches would themselves form an image to the beast; hence the enforcement of Sundaykeeping in the United States would be an enforcement of the worship of the beast and his image.

"But Christians of past generations observed the Sunday, supposing that in so doing they were keeping the Bible Sabbath; and there are now true Christians in every church, not excepting the Roman Catholic communion, who honestly believe that Sunday is the Sabbath of divine appointment. God accepts their sincerity of purpose and their integrity before Him. But when Sunday observance shall be enforced by law, and the world shall be enlightened concerning the obligation of the true Sabbath, then whoever shall transgress the command of God, to obey a precept which has no higher authority than that of Rome, will thereby honor popery above God. He is paying homage to Rome and to the power which enforces the institution ordained by Rome. He is worshipping the beast and his image. As men then reject the institution which God has declared to be the sign of His authority, and honor in its stead that which Rome has chosen as the token of her supremacy, they will thereby accept the sign of allegiance to Rome--'the mark of the beast.' And it is not until the issue is thus plainly set before the people, and they are brought to choose between the commandments of God and the commandments of men, that those who continue in transgression will receive 'the mark of the beast.'

"The most fearful threatening ever addressed to mortals is contained in the third angel's message. That must be a terrible sin which calls down the wrath of God unmingled with mercy. Men are not to be left in darkness concerning this important matter; the warning against this sin is to be given to the world before the visitation of God's judgments, that all may know why they are to be inflicted, and have opportunity to escape them. Prophecy declares that the first angel would make his announcement to 'every nation, and kindred, and tongue, and people.' The warning of the third angel, which forms a part of

58

the same threefold message, is to be no less widespread. It is represented in the prophecy as being proclaimed with a loud voice, by an angel flying in the midst of heaven; and it will command the attention of the world.

"In the issue of the contest all Christendom will be divided into two great classes--those who keep the commandments of God and the faith of Jesus, and those who worship the beast and his image and receive his mark. Although church and state will unite their power to compel 'all, both small and great, rich and poor, free and bond' (Revelation 13:16), to receive 'the mark of the beast,' yet the people of God will not receive it. The prophet of Patmos beholds 'them that had gotten the victory over the beast, and over his image, and over his mark, and over the number of his name, stand on the sea of glass, having the harps of God' and singing the song of Moses and the Lamb. Revelation 15: 2, 3." *Ibid*, pp. 448-450.

16
THE UNITED STATES IN PROPHECY

That the United States should be represented in prophecy should not seem strange to us or be a surprise. Were not other major world powers represented in prophecy--Babylon, Medo-Persia, Greece and pagan Rome? See Chapter 1, "The Historical Prophecies of Daniel."

Following the beast that "resembled a leopard" (Revelation 13:2), John "saw another beast, coming out of the earth. He had two horns like a lamb." Revelation 13:11. Both the appearance of this beast "like a lamb" and the manner of its rise "coming out of the earth" indicate that the nation which it represents is unlike those previously presented.

The beast symbols depicted in Daniel 7 were beasts of prey rising when "the four winds of heaven" were "churning up the great sea." Daniel 7:2. Winds are a symbol of strife. The "four winds of heaven" churning up the sea represent scenes of conquest and revolution by which nations and their armies attained to power.

The angel told John that "waters . . . are peoples, multitudes, nations and languages." Revelation 17:15.

The beast in Revelation 13:11 appears with "two horns like a lamb," not a beast of prey. It also was seen "coming out of the earth" instead of a churning sea. Here is represented a nation rising to power in territory previously unoccupied and growing up gradually and peacefully. This could not happen in the Old World represented by the beasts in Daniel 7. It must be found in the Western Continent.

What nation was rising to power following the leopardlike beast of Revelation 13:2 at the end of the 1260-year time period-- 1798 A.D.? One nation, and only one, meets the specification of this prophecy. It cannot represent other than the United States of America.

Speakers and historians represent the rise of this nation in similar words to those used in the prophecy. "A prominent writer, describing the rise of the United States, speaks of '*the mystery of her coming forth from vacancy*,' and says: 'Like a *silent seed* we grew into empire.'--G. A. Townsend, *The New World Compared With the Old*, page 462. A European journal in 1850 spoke of the United States as a wonderful empire, which was 'emerging,' and '*amid the silence of the earth* daily adding to its power and pride.'--The *Dublin Nation*. Edward Everett, in an oration on the Pilgrim founders of this nation, said: 'Did they look for a retired spot, inoffensive for its obscurity, and safe in its remoteness, where the little church of Leyden might enjoy the freedom of conscience? Behold the *mighty regions* over which, in *peaceful conquest*, . . . they have borne the banners of the cross!'--Speech delivered at Plymouth, Massachusetts, Dec. 22, 1824, page 11." *The Great Controversy*, pp. 440, 441.

The beast "had two horns like a lamb." A lamb represents youth, gentleness and innocence, a fitting description of the character of the United States in its early years of development. Among those who came to this country were many Christian exiles who determined to establish a government "upon the broad foundation of civil and religious liberty. Their views found place in the Declaration of Independence, which sets forth the great truth that 'all men are created equal' and endowed with the inalienable right to 'life, liberty, and the pursuit of happiness.' And the Constitution guarantees to the people the right of self-government, providing that representatives elected by the popular vote shall enact and administer the laws. Freedom of religious faith was also granted, every man being permitted to worship God according to the dictates of his conscience. Republicanism and Protestantism became the fundamental principles of the nation. These principles are the secret of its power and prosperity. The oppressed and downtrodden throughout Christendom have turned to this land with interest and hope. Millions have sought its shores, and the United States has risen to a place among the most powerful nations of the earth." *The Great Controversy,* p. 441.

The text continues by saying "but he spoke like a dragon. He exercised all the authority of the first beast . . . whose fatal wound had been healed. . . . He ordered them to set up an image in honor of the beast who was wounded by the sword and yet lived." Revelation 13:11-14.

"The lamblike horns and dragon voice of the symbol point to a striking contradiction between the professions and the practice of the nation thus represented. The 'speaking' of the nation is the action of its legislative and judicial authorities. By such action it will give the lie to those liberal and peaceful principles which it has put forth as the foundation of its policy. The prediction that it will speak 'as a dragon' and exercise 'all the power of the first beast' plainly foretells a development of the spirit of intolerance and persecution that was manifested by the nations represented by the dragon and the leopardlike beast. And the statement that the beast with two horns 'causeth the earth and them which dwell therein to worship the first beast' indicates that the authority of this nation is to be exercised in enforcing some observance which shall be an act of homage to the papacy.

"Such action would be directly contrary to the principles of this government, to the genius of its free institutions, to the direct and solemn avowals of the Declaration of Independence, and to the Constitution. The founders of the nation wisely sought to guard against the employment of secular power on the part of the church, with its inevitable result--intolerance and persecution. The Constitution provides that 'Congress shall make no law respecting an establishment of religion, or prohibiting the free exercise thereof,' and that 'no religious test shall ever be required as a qualification to any office of public trust under the United States.' Only in flagrant violation of these safeguards to the nation's liberty, can any religious observance be enforced by civil authority. But the inconsistency of such action is no greater than is represented in the symbol. It is the beast with lamblike horns--in profession pure, gentle, and harmless--that speaks as a dragon." *The Great Controversy*, p. 442.

17
THE FINAL WARNING

"After this I saw another angel coming down from heaven. He had great authority, and the earth was illuminated by his splendor. With a mighty voice he shouted: 'Fallen! Fallen is Babylon the Great! She has become a home for demons and a haunt for every evil spirit, a haunt for every unclean and detestable bird.' . . . Then I heard another voice from heaven say: 'Come out of her, my people, so that you will not share in her sins, so that you will not receive any of her plagues.'" Revelation 18:1, 2, 4.

"This scripture points forward to a time when the announcement of the fall of Babylon, as made by the second angel of Revelation 14 (verse 8), is to be repeated, with the additional mention of the corruptions which have been entering the various organizations that constitute Babylon, since that message was first given, in the summer of 1844." *The Great Controversy*, p. 603.

"Of Babylon, at the time brought to view in this prophecy, it is declared: 'Her sins have reached unto heaven, and God hath remembered her iniquities.' Revelation 18:5. She has filled up the measure of her guilt, and destruction is about to fall upon her. But God still has a people in Babylon; and before the visitation of His judgments these faithful ones must be called out, that they partake not of her sins and 'receive not of her plagues.' Hence the movement symbolized by the angel coming down from heaven, lightening the earth with his glory and crying mightily with a strong voice, announcing the sins of Babylon. In connection with his message the call is heard: 'Come out of her, My people.' These announcements, uniting with the third angel's message, constitute the final warning to be given to the inhabitants of the earth.

"Fearful is the issue to which the world is to be brought. The powers of earth, uniting to war against the commandments of God, will decree that 'all, both small and great, rich and poor, free and bond' (Revelation 13:16), shall conform to the customs of the church by the observance of the false sabbath. All who refuse compliance will be visited with civil penalties, and it will finally be declared that they are deserving of death. On the other hand, the law of God enjoining the Creator's rest day demands obedience and threatens wrath against all who transgress its precepts.

"With the issue thus clearly brought before him, whoever shall trample upon God's law to obey a human enactment receives the mark of the beast; he accepts the sign of allegiance to the power which he chooses to obey instead of God. The warning from heaven is: 'If any man worship the beast and his image, and receive his mark in his forehead, or in his hand, the same shall drink of the wine of the wrath of God, which is poured out without mixture into the cup of His indignation.' Revelation 14:9, 10.

"But not one is made to suffer the wrath of God until the truth has been brought home to his mind and conscience, and has been rejected. There are many who have never had an opportunity to hear the special truths for this time. The obligation of the fourth commandment has never been set before them in its true light. He who reads every heart and tries every motive will leave none who desire a knowledge of the truth, to be deceived as to the issues of the controversy. The decree is not to be urged upon the people blindly. Every one is to have sufficient light to make his decision intelligently.

"The Sabbath will be the great test of loyalty, for it is the point of truth especially controverted. When the final test shall be brought to bear upon men, then the line of distinction will be drawn between those who serve God and those who serve Him not. While the observance of the false sabbath in compliance with the law of the state, contrary to the fourth commandment, will be an avowal of allegiance to a power that is in opposition to God, the keeping of the true Sabbath, in obedience to God's law, is an evidence of loyalty to the Creator. While one class, by accepting the sign of submission to earthly powers, receive the mark of the beast, the other choosing the token of allegiance to divine authority, receive the seal of God." *Ibid,* pp. 604, 605.

"Thus the message of the third angel will be proclaimed. As the time comes for it to be given with greatest power, the Lord will work through humble instruments, leading the minds of those who consecrate themselves to His service. The laborers will be qualified rather by the unction of His Spirit than by the training of literary institutions. Men of faith and prayer will be constrained to go forth with holy zeal, declaring the words which God gives them. The sins of Babylon will be laid open. The fearful results of enforcing the observances of the church by civil authority, the inroads of spiritualism, the stealthy but rapid progress of the papal power--all will be unmasked. By these solemn warnings the people will be stirred. Thousands upon thousands will listen who have never heard words like these. In amazement they hear the testimony that Babylon is the church, fallen because of her errors and sins, because of her rejection of the truth sent to her from heaven. As the people go to their former teachers with the eager inquiry, Are these things so? the ministers present fables, prophesy smooth things, to soothe their fears and quiet the awakened conscience. But since many refuse to be satisfied with the mere authority of men and demand a plain 'Thus saith the Lord,' the popular ministry, like the Pharisees of old, filled with anger as their authority is questioned, will denounce the message as of Satan and stir up the sin-loving multitudes to revile and persecute those who proclaim it.

"As the controversy extends into new fields and the minds of the people are called to God's downtrodden law, Satan is astir. The power attending the message will only madden those who oppose it. The clergy will put forth almost superhuman efforts to shut away the light lest it should shine upon their flocks. By every means at their command they will endeavor to suppress the discussion of these vital questions. The church appeals to the strong arm of civil power, and, in this work, papists and Protestants unite. As the movement for Sunday enforcement becomes more bold and decided, the law will be invoked against commandment keepers." *Ibid,* pp. 606, 607. See Chapter 15, "The Message of the Third Angel."

It is during this final hour of earth's history before Jesus closes the Sanctuary in heaven and probation on earth ends, that we hear the closing remarks of the Father, the Son, the Holy Spirit and the apostle John. Please listen carefully.

From God the Father

"He who was seated on the throne said, 'I am making everything new!' Then he said, 'Write this down, for these words are trustworthy and true.' He said to me: 'It is done. I am the Alpha and the Omega, the Beginning and the End. To him who is thirsty I will give to drink without cost from the spring of the water of life. He who overcomes will inherit all this, and I will be his God and he will be my son. But the cowardly, the unbelieving, the vile, the murderers, the sexually immoral, those who practice magic arts, the idolaters and all liars--their place will be in the fiery lake of burning sulfur. This is the second death.'" Revelation 21:5-8.

From God the Son

"'Behold, I am coming soon! Blessed is he who keeps the words of the prophecy in this book.' . . . 'Behold, I am coming soon! My reward is with me, and I will give to everyone according to what he has done. I am the Alpha and the Omega, the First and the Last, the Beginning and the End. Blessed are those who wash their robes, that they may have the right to the tree of life and may go through the gates into the city. Outside are the dogs, those who practice magic arts, the sexually immoral, the murderers, the idolaters and everyone who loves and practices falsehood. I, Jesus, have sent my angel to give you this testimony for the churches. I am the Root and the Offspring of David, and the bright Morning Star.' . . . He who testifies to these things says, 'Yes, I am coming soon.'" Revelation 22:7, 12-16, 20.

From God the Holy Spirit

"The Spirit and the bride say, 'Come!' And let him who hears say, 'Come!' Whoever is thirsty, let him come; and whoever wishes, let him take the free gift of the water of life." Revelation 22:17.

From John the Apostle

"I, John, am the one who heard and saw these things. And when I had heard and seen them, I fell down to worship at the feet of the angel who had been showing them to me. But he said to me, 'Do not do it! I am a fellow servant with you and with your brothers the prophets and of all who keep the words of this book. Worship God!' Then he told me, 'Do not seal up the words of the prophecy of this book, because the time is near. Let him who does wrong continue to do wrong; let him who is vile continue to be vile; let him who does right continue to do right; and let him who is holy continue to be holy.' . . . I warn everyone who hears the words of the prophecy of this book: If anyone adds anything to them, God will add to him the plagues described in this book. And if anyone takes words away from this book of prophecy, God will take away from him his share in the tree of life and in the holy city, which are described in this book. . . . Amen. Come, Lord Jesus. The grace of the Lord Jesus be with God's people. Amen." Revelation 22:8-11, 18, 19, 20 (last part), 21.

18
THE WEDDING OF THE LAMB

"Let us rejoice and be glad and give him glory! For the wedding of the Lamb has come, and his bride has made herself ready." Revelation 19:7.

When the sanctuary in heaven closes there will be a great celebration. Revelation 19:1-10. "After this I heard what sounded like the roar of a great multitude in heaven shouting: 'Hallelujah! Salvation and glory and power belong to our God, for true and just are his judgments. He has condemned the great prostitute.'" Revelation 19:1, 2. These verses inform us that the investigation will then be complete and the great prostitute has been found guilty. For more information on the prostitute, see Chapter 14, "The Message of the Second Angel" and Chapter 17, "The Final Warning."

Upon completing the investigative judgment Christ is given authority to reign over His kingdom. John writes concerning Christ's reception of the kingdom: "For our Lord God Almighty reigns. . . . For the wedding of the Lamb has come, and his bride has made herself ready." "I saw the Holy City, the new Jerusalem, . . . prepared as a bride beautifully dressed for her husband." Revelation 19:6, 7; 21:2.

"The marriage represents the reception by Christ of His kingdom. The Holy City, the New Jerusalem, which is the capital and representative of the kingdom, is called 'the bride, the Lamb's wife.' Said the angel to John: 'Come hither, I will show thee the bride, the Lamb's wife.' 'He carried me away in the spirit,' says the prophet, 'and showed me that great city, the holy Jerusalem, descending out of heaven from God.' Revelation 21:9, 10. . . . In the Revelation the people of God are said to be the guests at the marriage supper. Revelation 19:9. If *guests*, they cannot be represented also as the *bride*. Christ, as stated by the prophet Daniel, will receive from the Ancient of Days in heaven, 'dominion, and glory, and a kingdom;' He will receive the New Jerusalem, the capital of His kingdom, 'prepared as a bride adorned for her husband.' Daniel 7:14; Revelation 21:2."*The Great Controversy,* pp. 426, 427.

Jesus Himself, in the parable of the wedding banquet recorded in Matthew 22, describes the church as guests who were invited to the wedding banquet. Matthew 22:11 says that the king (God) comes in to examine the guests to see if everyone has on the required garment. The wedding clothes are "the righteous acts of the saints." Revelation 19:8. These verses tell us that those who attend the wedding banquet must put on the character of Christ. Those who have not cooperated with God in developing Christ's character will be thrown out. Matthew 22:13.

The parable of the ten virgins in Matthew 25:1-10 is another wedding story. In this parable the church is represented as ten virgins who went out to meet the bridegroom and join the wedding party. Although we are not told who the bride is in this parable, clearly the wise virgins are not the bride because they join the wedding party as guests.

"In the Bible the sacred and enduring character of the relation that exists between Christ and His church is represented by the union of marriage. The Lord has joined His people to Himself by a solemn covenant, He promising to be their God, and they pledging themselves to be His and His alone." *The Great Controversy*, p. 381. We see that in the Scriptures the church is beautifully *represented* as the bride of Christ to *illustrate* the love that He has for His faithful followers.

"The followers of Christ are to 'wait for their Lord, when He will *return from* the wedding.' Luke 12:36." "They were not to be present in person at the marriage; for it takes place in heaven, while they are upon the earth. . . . But they are to understand His work, and to follow Him by faith as He goes in before God. It is in this sense that they are said to go in to the marriage." *Ibid*, p. 427. As we see in this quotation, the church is on earth while the wedding takes place in heaven. Those who have Christ's character are then invited to the wedding banquet, but they will not be present at the wedding itself.

The teaching that the bride in Revelation is the church is an error of greater significance than the deception of the early advent awakening in the 1840's in which the Christian world generally believed that the earth was the sanctuary to be cleansed when in truth it was the sanctuary in heaven that was to be cleansed. Let us not be deceived into thinking that because we belong to a church organization or make a profession of Christianity we are the bride of Christ and therefore we are saved regardless of how we live.

It is a solemn thought to realize that we are being examined now during the investigative judgment. This investigation will determine whether or not we have put on the wedding garment, the character of Christ. If we have put on the robe of His righteousness, we can attend the wedding supper of the Lamb of God in heaven.

THE BATTLE OF ARMAGEDDON

The last issue to come before the people of this world will be: "which day shall be our day of worship?" The confederacies of this world will, by law, say that Sunday, the first day of the week, shall be the day of worship for the whole world. On the other side of the controversy a small remnant of people will say that the seventh-day Sabbath is the day of worship required by the God of heaven in the ten commandments and upheld through all the Scriptures. See Chapter 15, "The Message of the Third Angel" and Chapter 17, "The Final Warning."

When everyone in the world has made their decision as to who they will obey, the God of heaven or the laws of men, then Christ will close His work in the Heavenly sanctuary. At this time the wedding of the Lamb takes place in heaven. See Chapter 18, "The Wedding of the Lamb."

The events on earth are of quite a different nature. The closing of the sanctuary in heaven is described in Revelation 15. There we are told "the temple was filled with smoke" and would remain closed "until the seven plagues . . . were completed." Revelation 15:8.

When the mediation of Jesus in the heavenly sanctuary closes, there will be no more sacrifice for sin; probation on earth will close and the plagues will begin to fall. About this time a law will be passed by the nations of earth setting a date on which to

6

kill all those who do not yield to the Sunday law but continue to worship on the seventh-day Sabbath. Revelation 13:15. It is then that the God of heaven will intervene to deliver His people. See Daniel 2:44, 45; 7:22, 26, 27; 8:25 (last part); Isaiah 30:29, 30.

John the Revelator describes the coming of Jesus at this time. Revelation 19:11-21. He sees Jesus "dressed in a robe dipped in blood" and the "armies of heaven were following him, riding on white horses." During the ensuing battle the fifth, sixth, and seventh plagues (Revelation 16:10-12, 17-21) are completed and the Battle of Armageddon is fought. "Then I saw the beast and the kings of the earth and their armies gathered together to make war against the rider on the horse and his army. But the beast was captured, and with him the false prophet who had performed the miraculous signs on his behalf. With these signs he had deluded those who had received the mark of the beast and worshiped his image. The two of them were thrown alive into the fiery lake of burning sulfur." Revelation 19:19, 20.

When this battle is over no living person is left on earth. The wicked are all dead and the saints are taken to heaven by the Rider on the white horse.

The apostle Paul states: "For the Lord himself will come down from heaven, with a loud command, with the voice of the archangel and with the trumpet call of God, and the dead in Christ will rise first. After that, we who are still alive and are left will be caught up together with them in the clouds to meet the Lord in the air. And so we will be with the Lord forever." I Thessalonians 4:16, 17.

Below is a simple diagram of the events occurring between the close of probation and the millennium.

A Study Guide On The Order Of Events
Close Of Probation To The Beginning Of The Millennium

Close of
Probation

Beginning of
Millennium

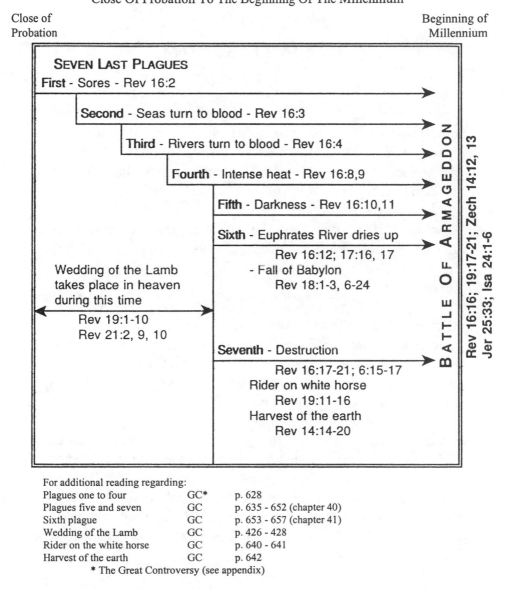

For additional reading regarding:

Plagues one to four	GC*	p. 628
Plagues five and seven	GC	p. 635 - 652 (chapter 40)
Sixth plague	GC	p. 653 - 657 (chapter 41)
Wedding of the Lamb	GC	p. 426 - 428
Rider on the white horse	GC	p. 640 - 641
Harvest of the earth	GC	p. 642

* The Great Controversy (see appendix)

20

THE MILLENNIUM

Today there is great interest and planning for the long-anticipated 1,000 years of peace which is expected to begin on this earth in 2000 A.D. But let us consider what the Scriptures say concerning the millennium (a Latin term which means a thousand years).

Revelation 20:1-7 mentions this one-thousand-year period six times. The following quotations give us a deeper insight into the events that occur at the beginning, during, and end of the thousand years.

"The revelator foretells the banishment of Satan and the condition of chaos and desolation to which the earth is to be reduced, and he declares that this condition will exist for a thousand years. After presenting the scenes of the Lord's second coming and the destruction of the wicked, the prophecy continues: 'I saw an angel come down from heaven, having the key of the bottomless pit and a great chain in his hand. And he laid hold on the dragon, that old serpent, which is the devil, and Satan, and bound him a thousand years, and cast him into the bottomless pit, and shut him up, and set a seal upon him, that he should deceive the nations no more, till the thousand years should be fulfilled: and after that he must be loosed a little season.' Revelation 20:1-3.

"That the expression 'bottomless pit' represents the earth in a state of confusion and darkness is evident from other scriptures. Concerning the condition of the earth 'in the beginning,' the Bible record says that it 'was without form, and void; and darkness was upon the face of the deep.' Genesis 1:2. Prophecy teaches that it will be brought back, partially at least, to this condition. Looking forward to the great day of God, the prophet Jeremiah declares: 'I beheld the earth, and, lo, it was without form, and void; and the heavens, and they had no light. I beheld the mountains, and, lo, they trembled, and all the hills moved lightly. I beheld, and, lo, there was no man, and all the birds of the heavens were fled. I beheld, and, lo, the fruitful place was a wilderness, and all the cities thereof were broken down.' Jeremiah 4:23-26.

"Here is to be the home of Satan with his evil angels for a thousand years. Limited to the earth, he will not have access to other worlds to tempt and annoy those who have never fallen. It is in this sense that he is bound: there are none remaining, upon whom he can exercise his power. He is wholly cut off from the work of deception and ruin which for so many centuries has been his sole delight." *The Great Controversy*, pp. 658, 659.

"For six thousand years, Satan's work of rebellion has 'made the earth to tremble.' He has 'made the world as a wilderness, and destroyed the cities thereof.' And he 'opened not the house of his prisoners.' [Isaiah 14:16, 17]. For six thousand years his prison house has received God's people, and he would have held them captive forever; but Christ has broken his bonds and set the prisoners free.

"Even the wicked are now placed beyond the power of Satan, and alone with his evil angels he remains to realize the effect of the curse which sin has brought. 'The kings of the nations, even

77

all of them, lie in glory, everyone in his own house [the grave]. But thou art cast out of thy grave like an abominable branch. . . . Thou shalt not be joined with them in burial, because thou hast destroyed thy land, and slain thy people.' Isaiah 14:18-20.

"For a thousand years, Satan will wander to and fro in the desolate earth to behold the results of his rebellion against the law of God. During this time his sufferings are intense. Since his fall his life of unceasing activity has banished reflection; but he is now deprived of his power and left to contemplate the part which he has acted since first he rebelled against the government of heaven, and to look forward with trembling and terror to the dreadful future when he must suffer for all the evil that he has done and be punished for the sins that he has caused to be committed." *Ibid*, pp. 659, 660.

"During the thousand years between the first and the second resurrection the judgment of the wicked takes place. The apostle Paul points to this judgment as an event that follows the second advent. 'Judge nothing before the time, until the Lord come, who both will bring to light the hidden things of darkness, and will make manifest the counsels of the hearts.' 1 Corinthians 4:5. Daniel declares that when the Ancient of Days came, 'judgment was given to the saints of the Most High.' Daniel 7:22. At this time the righteous reign as kings and priests unto God. John in the Revelation says: 'I saw thrones, and they sat upon them, and judgment was given unto them.' 'They shall be priests of God and of Christ, and shall reign with Him a thousand years.' Revelation 20:4, 6. It is at this time that, as foretold by Paul, 'the saints shall judge the world.' 1 Corinthians 6:2. In union with Christ they judge the wicked, comparing their acts with the statue book, the Bible, and deciding every case according to the deeds done in the body. Then the portion which the wicked must suffer is meted out, according to their works; and it is recorded against their names in the book of death.

"Satan also and evil angels are judged by Christ and His people. Says Paul: 'Know ye not that we shall judge angels?' Verse 3. And Jude declares that 'the angels which kept not their first estate, but left their own habitation, He hath reserved in everlasting chains under darkness unto the judgment of the great day.' Jude 6.

"At the close of the thousand years the second resurrection will take place. Then the wicked will be raised from the dead and appear before God for the execution of 'the judgment written.' Thus the revelator, after describing the resurrection of the righteous, says: 'The rest of the dead lived not again until the thousand years were finished.' Revelation 20:5. And Isaiah declares, concerning the wicked: 'They shall be gathered together, as prisoners are gathered in the pit, and shall be shut up in the prison, and *after many days shall they be visited.'* Isaiah 24:22. " *Ibid*, pp. 660, 661.

21
THE CONTROVERSY ENDED

Following the close of the one thousand years, John saw "the Holy City, the new Jerusalem, coming down out of heaven from God." Revelation 21:2. See also Revelation 21:10. The new Jerusalem is the capital of the Universe and the home of the saints who were taken to heaven at the beginning of the thousand years. See Revelation 20:6.

"Now Satan prepares for a last mighty struggle for the supremacy. While deprived of his power and cut off from his work of deception, the prince of evil was miserable and dejected; but as the wicked dead are raised and he sees the vast multitudes upon his side, his hopes revive, and he determines not to yield the great controversy. He will marshal all the armies of the lost under his banner and through them endeavor to execute his plans. . . . He proposes to lead them against the camp of the saints and to take possession of the City of God. With fiendish exultation he points to the unnumbered millions who have been raised from the dead and declares that as their leader he is well able to overthrow the city and regain his throne and his kingdom." *The Great Controversy*, p. 663.

Their work is soon interrupted and their attention is drawn to scenes involving the coronation of Christ.

"In the presence of the assembled inhabitants of earth and heaven the final coronation of the Son of God takes place. And now, invested with supreme majesty and power, the King of kings pronounces sentence upon the rebels against His government and executes justice upon those who have transgressed His law and oppressed His people. Says the prophet of God: 'I saw a great white throne, and Him that sat on it, from whose face the earth and the heaven fled away; and there was found no place for them. And I saw the dead, small and great, stand before God; and the books were opened: and another book was opened, which is the book of life: and the dead were judged out of those things which were written in the books, according to their works.' Revelation 20:11, 12.

"As soon as the books of record are opened, and the eye of Jesus looks upon the wicked, they are conscious of every sin which they have ever committed. They see just where their feet diverged from the path of purity and holiness, just how far pride and rebellion have carried them in the violation of the law of God. The seductive temptations which they encouraged by indulgence in sin, the blessings perverted, the messengers of God despised, the warnings rejected, the waves of mercy beaten back by the stubborn, unrepentant heart--all appear as if written in letters of fire.

"Above the throne is revealed the cross; and like a panoramic view appear the scenes of Adam's temptation and fall, and the successive steps in the great plan of redemption. The Saviour's lowly birth; His early life of simplicity and obedience; His baptism in Jordan; the fast and temptation in the wilderness; His public ministry, unfolding to men heaven's most precious blessings; the days crowded with deeds of love and mercy, the nights of prayer and watching in the solitude of the mountains; the plottings of envy, hate, and malice which repaid His benefits; the awful, mysterious agony in Gethsemane beneath

81

the crushing weight of the sins of the whole world; His betrayal into the hands of the murderous mob; the fearful events of that night of horror--the unresisting prisoner, forsaken by His best-loved disciples, rudely hurried through the streets of Jerusalem; the Son of God exultingly displayed before Annas, arraigned in the high priest's palace, in the judgment hall of Pilate, before the cowardly and cruel Herod, mocked, insulted, tortured, and condemned to die--all are vividly portrayed.

"And now before the swaying multitude are revealed the final scenes--the patient Sufferer treading the path to Calvary; the Prince of heaven hanging upon the cross; the haughty priests and the jeering rabble deriding His expiring agony; the supernatural darkness; the heaving earth, the rent rocks, the open graves, marking the moment when the world's Redeemer yielded up His life.

"The awful spectacle appears just as it was. Satan, his angels, and his subjects have no power to turn from the picture of their own work. Each actor recalls the part which he performed. Herod, who slew the innocent children of Bethlehem that he might destroy the King of Israel; the base Herodias, upon whose guilty soul rests the blood of John the Baptist; the weak, timeserving Pilate; the mocking soldiers; the priests and rulers and the maddened throng who cried, 'His blood be on us, and on our children!'--all behold the enormity of their guilt. They vainly seek to hide from the divine majesty of His countenance, outshining the glory of the sun, while the redeemed cast their crowns at the Saviour's feet, exclaiming: 'He died for me!'

"Amid the ransomed throng are the apostles of Christ, the heroic Paul, the ardent Peter, the loved and loving John, and their truehearted brethren, and with them the vast host of martyrs; while outside the walls, with every vile and abominable thing, are those by whom they were persecuted, imprisoned, and slain.

82

There is Nero, that monster of cruelty and vice, beholding the joy and exaltation of those whom he once tortured, and in whose extremest anguish he found satanic delight. His mother is there to witness the result of her own work; to see how the evil stamp of character transmitted to her son, the passions encouraged and developed by her influence and example, have borne fruit in crimes that caused the world to shudder.

"There are papist priests and prelates, who claimed to be Christ's ambassadors, yet employed the rack, the dungeon, and the stake to control the consciences of His people. There are the proud pontiffs who exalted themselves above God and presumed to change the law of the Most High. Those pretended fathers of the church have an account to render to God from which they would fain be excused. Too late they are made to see that the Omniscient One is jealous of His law and that He will in no wise clear the guilty. They learn now that Christ identified His interest with that of His suffering people; and they feel the force of His own words: 'Inasmuch as ye have done it unto one of the least of these My brethren, ye have done it unto Me.' Matthew 25:40.

"The whole wicked world stand arraigned at the bar of God on the charge of high treason against the government of heaven. They have none to plead their cause; they are without excuse; and the sentence of eternal death is pronounced against them." *Ibid,* pp. 666-668.

"The wicked receive their recompense in the earth. Proverbs 11:31. They 'shall be stubble: and the day that cometh shall burn them up, saith the Lord of hosts.' Malachi 4:1. Some are destroyed as in a moment, while others suffer many days. All are punished 'according to their deeds.' The sins of the righteous having been transferred to Satan, he is made to suffer not only for his own rebellion, but for all the sins which he has caused God's people to commit. His punishment is to be far greater than that of those whom he has deceived. After all have perished who fell by his deceptions, he is still to live and suffer on. In the cleansing flames the wicked are at last destroyed, root and branch--Satan the root, his followers the branches. The full penalty of the law has been visited; the demands of justice have been met; and heaven and earth, beholding, declare the righteousness of Jehovah.

"Satan's work of ruin is forever ended. For six thousand years he has wrought his will, filling the earth with woe and causing grief throughout the universe. The whole creation has groaned and travailed together in pain. Now God's creatures are forever delivered from his presence and temptations. 'The whole earth is at rest, and is quiet: they [the righteous] break forth into singing.' Isaiah 14:7. And a shout of praise and triumph ascends from the whole loyal universe. 'The voice of a great multitude,' 'as the voice of many waters, and as the voice of mighty thunderings,' is heard, saying: 'Alleluia: for the Lord God omnipotent reigneth.' Revelation 19:6." *Ibid*, p. 673.

"In the Bible the inheritance of the saved is called 'a country.' Hebrews 11:14-16. There the heavenly Shepherd leads His flock to fountains of living waters. The tree of life yields its fruit every month, and the leaves of the tree are for the service of the nations. There are ever-flowing streams, clear as crystal, and beside them waving trees cast their shadows upon the paths prepared for the ransomed of the Lord. There the wide-spreading plains swell into hills of beauty, and the mountains of God rear their lofty summits. On those peaceful plains, beside those living streams, God's people, so long pilgrims and wanderers, shall find a home.

"'My people shall dwell in a peaceable habitation, and in sure dwellings, and in quiet resting places.' 'Violence shall no more be heard in thy land, wasting nor destruction within thy borders; but thou shalt call thy walls Salvation, and thy gates Praise.' 'They shall build houses, and inhabit them; and they shall plant vineyards, and eat the fruit of them. They shall not build, and another inhabit; they shall not plant, and another eat: . . . Mine elect shall long enjoy the work of their hands.' Isaiah 32:18; 60:18; 65:21, 22.

"There, 'the wilderness and the solitary place shall be glad for them; and the desert shall rejoice, and blossom as the rose.' 'Instead of the thorn shall come up the fir tree, and instead of the brier shall come up the myrtle tree.' 'The wolf also shall dwell with the lamb, and the leopard shall lie down with the kid; . . . and a little child shall lead them.' 'They shall not hurt nor destroy in all My holy mountain,' saith the Lord. Isaiah 35:1; 55:13; 11:6, 9.

"Pain cannot exist in the atmosphere of heaven. There will be no more tears, no funeral trains, no badges of mourning. 'There shall be no more death, neither sorrow, nor crying: . . . for the former things are passed away.' 'The inhabitant shall not say, I am sick: the people that dwell therein shall be forgiven their iniquity.' Revelation 21:4; Isaiah 33:24.

"There is the New Jerusalem, the metropolis of the glorified new earth, 'a crown of glory in the hand of the Lord, and a royal diadem in the hand of thy God.' 'Her light was like unto a stone most precious, even like a jasper stone, clear as crystal.' 'The nations of them which are saved shall walk in the light of it· and the kings of the earth do bring their glory and honor into it.' Saith the Lord: 'I will rejoice in Jerusalem, and joy in My people.' 'The tabernacle of God is with men, and He will dwell with them, and they shall be His people, and God Himself shall be with them, and be their God.' Isaiah 62:3; Revelation 21:11, 24; Isaiah 65:19; Revelation 21:3.

"In the City of God 'there shall be no night.' None will need or desire repose. There will be no weariness in doing the will of God and offering praise to His name. We shall ever feel the freshness of the morning and shall ever be far from its close. 'And they need no candle, neither light of the sun; for the Lord God giveth them light.' Revelation 22:5. The light of the sun will be superseded by a radiance which is not painfully dazzling, yet which immeasurably surpasses the brightness of our noontide. The glory of God and the Lamb floods the Holy City with unfading light. The redeemed walk in the sunless glory of perpetual day.

"'I saw no temple therein: for the Lord God Almighty and the Lamb are the temple of it.' Revelation 21:22. The people of God are privileged to hold open communion with the Father and the Son. 'Now we see through a glass, darkly.' 1 Corinthians 13:12. We behold the image of God reflected, as in a mirror, in the works of nature and in His dealings with men; but then we shall see Him face to face, without a dimming veil between. We shall stand in His presence and behold the glory of His countenance." *Ibid*, pp. 675-677.

"The great controversy is ended. Sin and sinners are no more. The entire universe is clean. One pulse of harmony and gladness beats through the vast creation. From Him who created all, flow life and light and gladness, throughout the realms of illimitable space. From the minutest atom to the greatest world, all things, animate and inanimate, in their unshadowed beauty and perfect joy, declare that God is love." *Ibid,* p. 678.

APPENDIX

Page 75. For more information regarding the first four plagues, see Ellen G. White, *The Great Controversy Between Christ and Satan*, p. 628.

Available from

Revelation Ministry
P.O. Box 184
Days Creek, Oregon 97429
(541) 8225-3538

or

CHJ Publishing
1103 West Main
Middleton, Idaho 83644
(208) 585-2602